HOW TO BUY A
GOOD BUSINESS
WITH LITTLE OR NONE
OF YOUR OWN MONEY

"HOW TO BUY A GOOD BUSINESS

WITH LITTLE OR NONE OF YOUR OWN MONEY

Lionel Haines

𝕿imes BOOKS

Library of Congress Cataloging-in-Publication Data
Haines, Lionel.
  How to buy a good business with little or none of your
  own money.

  Includes index.
  1. Leveraged buyouts.   I. Title.
HD2746.5.H35   1987   658.1′6   86-30017
ISBN 0-8129-1627-1

Manufactured in the United States of America

Designed by
Melissa Feldman and Naomi Osnos

BOMC offers recordings and compact discs, cassettes
and records. For information and catalog write to
BOMR, Camp Hill, PA 17012.

To my wife, business partner and best friend,
Henrietta,
whose love made this possible

■Contents

1. How to Buy a Good Business with Little or
    None of Your Own Money   3

2. How to Find the Right Deal   19

3. How to Tell If It's Right   39

4. How Much Is It Worth?   69

5. How to Structure the Deal   84

6. How to Finance the Deal   111

7. How to Negotiate the Deal   133

8. How to Close the Deal   152

9. How to Survive Your First Year   167

Appendix: Due Diligence Checklist   177

Index   203

HOW TO BUY A
GOOD BUSINESS
WITH LITTLE OR NONE
OF YOUR OWN MONEY

How to Buy a Good Business with Little or None of Your Own Money

If you have ever said, "I'd love to have my own business but I don't have any money!" this book is for you.

I will show you how you can obtain significant wealth and financial security by buying a going business with little or none of your own money. I mean a solid, successful business that could provide you with an owner's income of $250,000 a year. I will show you how to get a good established business that will literally pay for itself—down payment and monthly installments—using the same techniques that made T. Boone Pickens, Ted Turner and Carl Icahn rich and famous.

Sound impossible? Well, it is being done every day by people just like you. So leave your doubt aside and welcome to the world of the leveraged buyout.

It was Archimedes, the Greek philosopher and mathematician, who said, "Give me a lever long enough and I will move the world," and I'm going to show you how you can use the principles of financial leverage to move yourself into the world of significant wealth and financial security.

You already know what leverage is. When you buy a home, you make a small down payment and borrow the rest. That is using leverage. It is just a fancy way of saying "other people's money." When you use other people's money to buy a business, it is called a leveraged buyout, or LBO. You do a leveraged buyout by using the assets and cash flow of the business to finance the entire purchase price—both the down payment and the monthly installments. The business buys itself. And you own it.

If you are like most people, the first time you encounter this idea, you have three basic questions: "Why would I want to buy a business?" "Who would sell me a good business if I have no money and poor credit?" and "Can I really do it?" These are fair questions and should be answered one at a time.

Why Buy a Business?

Financial security is a big part of the American dream. Nearly everyone is putting a little money away, saving up to buy a house or start a business, have a nice car, help the kids through school and retire in comfort. But the truth is that you cannot save your way to significant wealth for two reasons. First, the people who run the banks, insurance companies and other financial institutions where you save make their living by investing your money. After they take their profit not much is left for you. Just compare the interest rate you pay on your credit cards with the rate you get for your savings account.

Second, the dollars you do manage to squeeze out of your already overstretched budget are after-tax dollars. It is the combined forces of taxes and the profits of the financial middlemen that make it nearly impossible to save your way into the American dream. So you take your life savings and open your own business just as millions of Americans have done.

You can almost see it now. Your own business with your name on the door. After all, there are 14.5 million businesses in America. Any fool can run a business. You know that for a fact because you have worked for some of them. It is a wonderful dream, but the odds are against you. The reality is that 50 percent of all new businesses fail in their first year. By the end of the second year, 70 percent have closed their doors. And by the end of the fifth year, nine out of ten new business startups have gone belly up. However, you do not have to start a business to be in business. There is a better way.

It is cheaper, faster, smarter and safer to buy a good business than to start one. There are many reasons why this is true, but the bottom line is cash flow. When you start a business do you have cash flow? Sure you do. The cash flows from your pocket and out the door. Think about it for a moment. You are going to go into competition with me. I have been in business for twenty years. I have customers. I have a proven location. I have an established reputation. I have credit from my suppliers. I have all of these things in a going business that you will not have if you start a business. How long does it take you and how much does it cost you to build your business up to the point where mine is today?

Now I am not saying that you should not start a business if you really want to. I am pointing out that the odds are significantly against you. There are opportunities today to start significant new businesses. You may have a proprietary piece of technology. You may have spotted a market niche in which you can offer some goods or services better, cheaper or faster than anyone else, and you may succeed. But the odds are against you if you are starting a business. That is why I say it is cheaper, faster, smarter and safer to buy a good business rather than to start one. If you buy a good business today, you have cash flowing in tomorrow. And much of it can be yours, to keep.

Owners of successful small businesses frequently take home as much as $250,000 a year in salary, profits and perks or fringe benefits. Perks average $30,000 to $50,000 a year for small-business owners. And these are pretax dollars. The perks get written off as legitimate business expenses before taxes. Typically, these perks include cars, business trips to resort areas, boats, airplanes, club memberships, interest-free loans for home purchase or education of children, comprehensive insurance programs, and fully funded pension programs. (As an employee, you would pay for these goodies out of your salary after taxes have been deducted.) And these benefits are in addition to the value of the business itself, which now belongs to you.

If you buy a successful business for $1 million, you own a significant asset that produces a regular income. It does not matter that you buy the business with other people's money. In five to seven years, when the financing is paid off, you will own a $1 million business asset free and clear. It is yours. And it did not cost you a dime of your own money to get started. That's why you would want to buy a good business.

Who Would Sell Me a Good Business?

Where would you look for a good business if you did decide to buy one? Let's take a look at the structure of business in the United States. There are 14.5 million businesses in America. They are organized into a pyramid-shaped structure. Up at the top of that pyramid we have the 160,000 large corporations. Down at the base of the pyramid there are more than 10 million mom-and-pop shops: the small operations on the corner with one to three employees that make up the bulk of American businesses. Right there in the middle are 4.5 million businesses with annual sales of between $500,000 and $10 million. Now, among these businesses in this middle market the turnover is about 3 percent a year: so about 135,000 of these businesses are sold each year. Fully 15 percent, or 20,250, of those sales are leveraged buyouts. That's right, about 20,000 good businesses with sales of $500,000 to $10 million are sold each year to people who have very little or no money of their own in the deal. They acquired these businesses based entirely upon the assets and cash flow of the businesses themselves. And next year, one of them could be yours.

Another important thing to remember about the 4.5 million businesses in the middle market is that somewhere around 85 percent of them are fourteen years old or older. You are looking here at essentially well-established businesses.

The LBO candidate is not the exciting, rapid-growth company that larger corporations want to acquire. The LBO candidate is a solid, steady company with predictable sales and earnings that keep up with inflation but not much more. It is not a corporate acquisition target. Most of these kinds of businesses—over 100,000 of them each year—are liquidated because their owners had no exit plan. And three out of every four were ideal LBO candidates.

Where exactly will you begin to look for your first LBO? In this middle market of companies there are basically three types of LBO candidates:

• Divestitures of divisions of smaller companies by their larger corporate parent. These will be divisions or even product lines that the corporation has decided to spin off, either because they do not fit into the strategy of the company any longer or because they do not show sufficient profit. Business cycles are subject to fads in the same way that dress styles are. During the sixties the fad in business management was to acquire, diversify and form a conglomerate. It did not work out quite as well as some thought it would. During the late seventies many of these same companies began spinning off their smaller, less profitable or ill-fitting operations. This trend continues today, and these divestitures are a regular source of LBO candidates. For example, American Can Company has spun off ninety divisions, product lines or smaller companies within the last ten years and plans to spin off another twenty-seven in the next five years.

• Smaller public companies, those companies that went public in order to raise money or provide some liquidity for their owners. Basically, these are companies that never realized their early promise. So the shareholders, particularly the few shareholders that control the majority of the stock, have no path to liquidity. The stock price—and this is the kind of company you hear about in the penny markets —is probably languishing somewhere around ten cents a share, and the owners would love someone to come along, buy them out and take the company private.

• The privately held company sold by an individual seller. This last category is where you are going to find your LBO because the psychology of the seller works in your favor.

The Typical LBO Candidate

Let us take a look at the typical company of this type and its owner, the entrepreneur, who will be the typical seller of an LBO. Basically you are going to look for an individual who is a founder-entrepreneur; the man who started his own company. He will be between fifty-five and sixty-five years of age. He will have been in business fifteen to twenty-five years. The two most significant things about his business will be that the earnings have been flat and there will be very little debt. Mentally, this entrepreneur retired from his business about six or seven years ago. These are not unsuccessful businesses. These businesses will be profitable even if the earnings are flat. You will find that, typically, the profits last year were $100,000, the year before probably $97,000, the year before that probably $95,000, but they have been barely keeping up with inflation. LBO candidates will not have the exciting, stair-step growth that makes a company a hot prospect to go public or to be the acquisition candidate for a major corporation.

The company should show little or no debt (just as if you had owned your home for fifteen to twenty-five years and had greatly reduced or paid off the mortgage). It is in the nature of the entrepreneur of this generation to be very proud of the fact that he owns his business free and clear. When you finally meet some of these candidates you will hear them say, "I own it all, free and clear." And that is one of the tips you file away mentally that lets you know you are dealing with a real LBO candidate.

Let's leave the realm of statistics and abstractions for a moment and look at an actual example. Sam is sixty years old. He has been in business for twenty years. In 1945, at the age of twenty, he was discharged from the U.S. Army. He took his G.I. benefits and went to college, got a degree in mechanical engineering from Ohio State, married, worked his way up through a succession of jobs because he was a very good mechanical engineer, had a couple of kids, moved to the suburbs. Sam wanted his piece of the American dream. He wanted his kids to have the best education they could get. He wanted a nice house and a good car. He wanted it all just like he saw on television every night.

Time passed. It got to be 1965. Sam's kids were in high school, ready to go to college. He looked at the reports and saw that the two best universities in the United States were Harvard and the University of California, Berkeley. Since he wanted the best education for his kids, he decided to send them off—one to each. Sam knew that he was not going to realize the dream as an employee. So Sam took the plunge that millions of Americans have taken and started his own business. Most entrepreneurs are technicians, the people who know how to get things done. They go into business for the independence, wealth and financial security.

Sam was successful because he was a good mechanical engineer. He started his business in 1965 in the middle of the greatest continuing expansion in the American economy in the last fifty years. This was an uptrend that lasted for eight and a half years. You would have had to be a very bad businessman not to succeed during this period. But Sam was very good. His business grew to the point where he was grossing $3 million a year. He was taking home a salary of $200,000 a year and his perks, all those wonderful things like his car, his airplane, his country club membership and the vacations to the trade association meetings in Bermuda and the Bahamas, came to another $50,000 a year. And, remember, those are pretax dollars.

Also Sam's company was making a pretax net profit of about \$250,000 to \$270,000 a year. Sam was doing very well. The son, who had gone off to Harvard, decided to pursue a career as an off-Broadway playwright. The daughter, who went to the University of California, Berkeley, in the late sixties, became involved in the antiwar movement and is now working as an aide to a senator in Washington, D.C. Neither one of them is interested in running a very small, successful sheet metal company.

Sam is sixty now. He has no one to turn the reins over to, and he is tired. He has been doing the same thing for twenty years. It has come to the point where Sam only makes it into the office three days a week. He loves to go out to his country club and play a round with his suppliers and customers. Mentally he has retired from his business. He is no longer putting energy into making it grow. It dawns on him that there is nobody to take it over. "I'm not enjoying doing it and I really do want to retire. I might as well sell it. After all, it's a good, safe, predictable business." It is that very safety, that very steady predictability of Sam's business that really means the earnings are flat.

When Sam calls a local investment banker to find someone to acquire his business, he discovers that his business is just not an exciting acquisition candidate. The investment banker tells him, "Sam, the companies that are acquiring smaller companies are looking for rapid growth in earnings. You're already past that stairstep of rapid earnings growth, the sex appeal of a company on its way up. A company with flat earnings in a dull industry like sheet metal just isn't going to go." After Sam hears this from four or five different sources, he is hurt, he is dejected. He spent his lifetime building up a successful business and now nobody wants it. So in a fit of pique Sam decides he is going to put the key in the lock and walk away. He will simply liquidate the business.

From the moment Sam makes a commitment to liquidating his business, time is his enemy and the issue is confidentiality. Sam, like most entrepreneurs, has a significant portion of his net worth tied up in his business. Yes, he has his home and he has a fully funded pension plan, but that $3-million-a-year business represents the bulk of Sam's worldly wealth. That $3-million-a-year business has a net worth—that is the assets: his equipment, his fixtures, his inventory, his accounts receivable, minus the little bit of money he owes, of about $600,000.

When he begins to explore liquidating his business, he finds what so many retailers find in those weeks after Christmas—inventory on sale does not have much value. If you are liquidating your inventory, your equipment, your fixtures, your vehicles, you are going to be very lucky to get twenty or thirty cents on the dollar. But let us give Sam the benefit of the doubt here. Let us say that he is the most fortunate entrepreneur in the United States and that he realizes a full fifty cents on the dollar for his net worth. He can't be too happy about that. In liquidation his $600,000 net worth turns into $300,000. And that is only the beginning.

Time is Sam's enemy and the issue is confidentiality. This issue of confidentiality is why you do not find the really good LBO candidates in the Sunday newspaper ads or with your local Biz Op broker. From the moment Sam decides to sell, his business begins to deteriorate in value. It is going to take him six, nine, possibly twelve months to complete that liquidation. It is not going to happen overnight. It is a long, slow process.

The first thing Sam has to deal with are his employees. In his $3-million-a-year business, Sam has fifty or sixty employees. Many of these employees have been with Sam since the beginning. They came to work, put in long hours for low wages. These are his friends. He is a godfather to some of their children. In a few cases he has loaned them money to buy houses. Now he is going to walk away from all of them. Now Sam is going to tell them, "I've decided to retire. I'll give you a good recommendation. I know you won't have any trouble finding another job."

But Sam has a problem that he has not even thought about. Sam, like most entrepreneurs, does not have written personnel policies. Specifically, he does not have a written "use it or lose it" policy covering unused vacation time and sick leave. They simply have to come to him and say, "I haven't used it. I want to be paid for it," and he is obligated to do so. So Sam has an off–balance sheet liability to those fifty or sixty employees for $75,000 to $100,000 in unused vacation and sick days. Where is that money going to come from? It is going to come out of the $300,000 he got for his assets in liquidation.

But Sam is not out the door yet. The moment he tells his employees that he is going to liquidate his business, what do they do? They start preparing their résumés. They take time to look for jobs. Where do they go? They walk right out the door with all of Sam's business secrets, all of his connections and contacts, and go right to the competition. And the best employees leave first.

But Sam still is not out the door. Sam has customers. That was the reason he went into business in the first place —all of those wonderful customers paying their bills. Many of his customers have been with Sam from the beginning. They sometimes ordered more than they needed. They sometimes prepaid their invoices when Sam was going through tough times. They helped him out. Now he is going to them and he is going to say, "I'm shutting down my business and going to Arizona to do a little fishing." They are going to say, "Wonderful, Sam! We've enjoyed all these years of playing golf with you." But as soon as Sam walks out the door, they are going to tell their purchasing agents to look around for another supplier because Sam is going out of business.

The issue with the customers is recourse. One of the reasons you do business with Sam is because if anything goes wrong you can go back to him. If it does not fit, if it is not the right color, if it is damaged in transit, you have recourse. If he is liquidating his business, you do not know how much longer you are going to have that recourse. Instead of thinking of Sam as a primary supplier, he becomes a secondary supplier. The number of orders over this six- to twelve-month liquidation period begins to decrease. What happens to the payment of Sam's invoices? If Sam is no longer a key supplier, those bills that used to be paid in thirty days are now paid in forty-five days. The forty-five-day terms get stretched out to sixty and even to ninety days. Sam's cash flow is going down. And, as his customers find other suppliers, his orders are going down.

And he still is not out the door, because Sam has suppliers. Sam, like most entrepreneurs, built his business on the backs of his suppliers. They extended him credit. They stretched out their terms when Sam was experiencing difficulty. Now Sam is going to go to the same suppliers that he plays golf with two or three times a week and tell them he has decided to liquidate his business. The first thing they are going to do is take a look at his account to see the balance due. Then they are going to move the terms up. Sam is about to find out that he can no longer get goods on forty-five-day terms. It is not unusual in liquidation situations to find the entrepreneur confronted with a COD situation. The suppliers will continue to service him, but he is no longer a preferred customer. What about out-of-stock situations? Sam used to be able to count on getting whatever he needed when he needed it. Now, if there is a conflict, those key suppliers are going to go with their preferred customers. After all, Sam is going out of business. He is yesterday's news.

And Sam is *still* not out the door, because he has to face the loss of his perks: that $50,000 in indirect compensation, including the membership in the country club, the private plane, his Mercedes-Benz, his wife's Mercedes, the trips to Bermuda, the Bahamas and Hawaii on trade association junkets. He is going to lose all of those. Moreover, if he tries to provide those for himself out of his fully funded pension plan, he is going to find that he is paying for them with aftertax dollars instead of pretax dollars. That $50,000 perk package is going to cost Sam, the retired man, $100,000, where it cost Sam, the business owner, only $50,000. He is going to lose all of those perks, and he has come to love those vacations and those three or four days a week down at the country club. To repeat, from the time Sam said that he was going to liquidate his business, he began to lower the value of that business. Time is Sam's enemy and confidentiality is the issue. Once employees, customers and suppliers know the business is going to be liquidated, the value declines.

Now you, as an LBO buyer, come to Sam and you offer Sam the following alternative. You say, "Sam, not only am I going to see that you get the full $600,000 value of your net worth out of this company, but I'm going to show you an upside of another $400,000. As for your customers, I'm going to keep them. I want your customers—that's why I'm buying your business. Your employees? I'm going to keep them all. I want your solid, trained organization. I'm not interested in four walls and a roof. Your suppliers? I'm going to keep your suppliers. I don't want to reinvent the wheel. I don't want to go through the time and effort to build up a good credit rating. I want your suppliers. And, Sam, the best news of all: I'm going to show you a way that you can keep most of your perks." Sam would have to be nuts to liquidate his business in the face of an offer like that. And that is exactly why LBOs are done in the middle market. Sam, like so many entrepreneurs, became a candidate for a leveraged buyout because he has been so busy over the years trying to stay in business that he never planned his own exit from the business. You are his exit plan.

Is Sam really typical? Are there owners of businesses who would sell you their businesses even though you had little or none of your own money in the deal? The answer is yes. But first you must find the right owner with the right motive. There are dozens of reasons to sell a good business. The main reason is boredom—burnout—just being tired of doing the same thing for fifteen, twenty or twenty-five years. It is the number-one reason a seller sells his business. If the owner is fifty-five to sixty-five years old, then age and health can become significant factors. The fact is that one out of every two marriages in the United States ends in divorce. When you consider that business partners spend more time together than many marriage partners do, it is not surprising to find that divorce and partnership dissolution are high on the list of motives for selling good, solid businesses. Another motive is family—I have already described Sam's situation, but there are many people who do not want to do what their fathers did, and family reasons account for the sale of many businesses.

There are some important financial reasons for selling as well. Most entrepreneurs find that they have spent most of their adult lives building an asset that represents a significant portion of their net worth. It simply is not prudent for them, as they get into the fifty-five- to sixty-five-year age range, to have that much of their net worth in a single asset. It is time for them to think seriously about retirement and diversification. If you look at the $600,000 net worth in Sam's business, the return on his investment shows that Sam is paying a premium to own a job. If he took that $600,000 and invested it in tax-exempt municipal securities, he would be making about the same return free and clear of taxes without risk. It is not a good proposition for Sam to be paying a premium to own a job.

A motivated seller sells his business for emotional reasons and then rationalizes the decision. After all, the business, for many of these sellers, is their baby. They have put so much of their time and attention into building the business over the years that the thought of selling it is very much like the thought of giving up a child for adoption.

15

That is the emotional reality. And the emotional reality of selling has to precede the intellectual rationalization. That is why the real seller is looking for a real buyer—someone who will not destroy his business. It is not unusual to find sellers of businesses in the middle market putting into the contract for sale something called an "immortality clause." Typically it says: "My name on the door, the Tom Smith Company, is going to remain on the door for ten, fifteen, twenty years." This is their way of perpetuating their own immortality.

Summing It Up

The typical LBO candidate is between fifty-five and sixty-five years old. He has owned his business for fifteen to twenty-five years. It has flat earnings and very little debt. And he has lost interest in making it grow.

There are dozens of reasons to sell a good business; retirement and relocation, death, divorce and partnership disputes are among them. But the number-one reason is that the owner is tired, bored, burned out and ready to move on.

Once the typical LBO candidate realizes that his company is not going to be acquired by a large corporation, he faces the agony of actual liquidation. He is going to tell his employees, customers and suppliers of twenty years that he is locking the doors and walking away. Many of these people are close friends, more like family members. And he will have to face them for the six months to a year that it will take to sell off the assets of his business: the machinery, fixtures, equipment, vehicles, real estate and remaining inventory. If he is lucky, he may sell these assets for as much as 50 percent of their fair market value because he is liquidating and cannot get top dollar for them. That is why it is called the agony of actual liquidation.

Now, consider the alternative—the leveraged buyout —which you are going to offer the seller. After negotiations, Sam agrees to take $1 million for his business on your terms. And the best part of the deal is that, with your terms, Sam is going to be able to keep about eighty cents of every dollar. So Sam will get $800,000 for his $1 million business, not the $125,000 he would get in a liquidation.

More money in the seller's pocket, that is why nearly 20,000 leveraged buyouts are done each year involving good, profitable businesses. It makes bottom line dollars and sense to the seller. He gets more for his business assets than he would from a liquidation without the personal agony of closing the doors. He gets to keep more after taxes. That is why sellers will sell good businesses to buyers who have no money and poor credit. The problem is not a lack of willing sellers. The problem is a lack of knowledgeable buyers, real buyers.

Can I Do It?

The real seller, the person who is going to sell you his business as a leveraged buyout, is looking for a real buyer. Are you a real buyer? Do you sincerely want to buy a good, successful business using little or none of your own money? You must begin by defining what you want. What are your personal objectives in buying a successful business? Are you trying to accumulate wealth or are you looking for financial security? Are you looking for investment diversification or do you simply want to run your own show? You must have your own personal objectives clearly in mind before you begin the active search for your first leveraged buyout candidate.

If you have the motivation and determination to own your own business, you can do it. I will show you how. The following chapters take you step by step through the process of doing your first LBO on your own. Every aspect is covered, from finding the right business to the final close of escrow. This book assumes no prior knowledge. It requires no special skills or training. It is a complete, comprehensive action guide. When you finish this book, you will know what to do next.

This is not just another motivational "get rich quick" scheme. It is long, hard work. It may take six to nine months to find the right business, check it out, negotiate a good deal with the owner and close escrow. You could invest 300 to 400 hours. But when it is over, you will own your own business.

This book is not another academic text. It is filled with practical, useful information gathered over twenty-five years of business and deal-making experience. This system works. I know. I have used it successfully for years. And it has worked for thousands of others.

2

How to Find the Right Deal

The search for the right business begins with the selection of the right industry.

That is so important I want to repeat it.

The search for the right business begins with the selection of the right industry. In looking for your first LBO it is best to select an industry in which you have some experience. You should either have worked in the industry, already own a business in that industry or have some real working knowledge from friends and family members who come from that industry. It may be a trade that you have picked up in the service. You are going to find that you have more credibility and a greater feeling of security if you stick to an industry where you have actual experience or some knowledge. You don't need to be an expert, but you should not be a complete beginner.

You should select an industry that is at least ten years old. You really want to find an industry that is at least fifteen to twenty-five years old; just as you are looking for businesses that are about fifteen to twenty-five years old. You do not want to get caught up in a fad. You want to avoid the next Hula-Hoop. If the industry has not really proven itself, you may find in a few years, when you are ready to sell, that there is no one around who's buying. Whenever you get into a business you should know how you are going to get out. You do not want to become the entrepreneur who stayed at the party too long. The need for an exit plan makes it crucial that you choose an established industry.

Furthermore, you can find out more about an established industry in which the procedures, techniques and margins have been worked out than you can about a new one. You can find out what the operating norms and standard ratios are for businesses in an established industry. You can determine how much is spent, typically, on advertising and sales commissions or whether sales are made directly by the company's own sales force or through independent manufacturer's representatives. All of these issues have been worked out in an established industry.

Industries have trends. They are either going up or going down. You should be looking for an industry that has been going up for at least the last three years. If your analysis of the industry indicates that the industry has hit a plateau and leveled off, the chances are you have not done enough homework. No industry remains flat. Industries are either on their way up or on their way down. If you have found an industry that has reached a plateau, do a little more homework. Find out whether you are really looking at an industry pausing for advance or decline.

Another issue that is very important in the selection of the right industry is whether the industry is consolidated or fragmented. By a consolidated industry I mean one like the automobile industry. Automobile manufacturing in the United States is dominated by the Big Three. Compare this situation with the furniture industry. Furniture manufacturing in the United States is a fragmented industry characterized by many small and medium-size competitors in local markets, each serving defined niches. In a consolidated industry, you have the problem of the industry leaders establishing pricing. They also determine turnover of products, product life cycles and many other key factors. You could find your business dancing to their tune. In a fragmented industry, you are more likely to be able to acquire a business that is a leader in a particular market niche. It may be difficult to find a company with gross annual revenues of $500,000 to $10 million that dominates a market niche, but that is what you should be looking for—a dominant position in a fragmented industry.

Where do you begin your analysis of an industry? I have found that the best place to begin an industry analysis is with the trade journals and newsletters in that industry. If you are not already familiar with all of the newsletters and trade journals in the industry that you have selected, go to a local library. Pick up a copy of *Business Rates and Data—Part I,* published by Standard Rate & Data Service, and go through it. You will find over 16,000 different trade journals organized by industry. It is a very small or very new industry that does not have at least one or two journals. Some of the major industries have three, four or five journals. The listing in *Rates and Data* will tell you not only where the publication is located but also the names of its key personnel. You want to know not only the phone number but also the name of the publisher, the editor, and if they are listed, the advertising manager and the senior editors.

You are going to contact every one of these trade journals and newsletters. You contact the publishers, editors, advertising managers and any senior editors and ask them about their industry. Pretend that you know nothing about the industry. Ask the questions you would ask if you were just beginning to explore the industry. Take your knowledge and experience and park it on the shelf. Let them tell you what they think about their industry in order for you to develop an objective picture.

Your approach should be simple and direct. Get through to the person with whom you wish to speak. Introduce yourself and tell this person that you are interested in buying a business in the industry. Ask for a minute or two of his or her time to explore general trends in the industry. When you find the people who want to talk, keep asking follow-up questions. Let them help you. It makes them feel good to be the expert and know that they are valued for their knowledge.

Why do I suggest going to the editor and the publisher, as well as the advertising manager and any senior editors? Is is because each will have a different perspective. The publisher of a magazine is far more likely to have an overview of the industry, while the editor is much more likely to be familiar with the current issues in the industry. The advertising manager will be familiar with the plans for growth or reduction. Senior editors who have been in the industry for fifteen or twenty years know the ins and outs, the names of the players, who is available and who is going where. From these conversations you will be able to develop an accurate picture of the future of the industry.

When you are asking your questions, you will want to focus on the most recent three years of history and on the next five years. What are the major issues? What is the structure of the industry? Where is it going over the next five years? It will be useful if you develop a list of questions before you begin and ask each of the individuals the same questions, in the same way, to make as objective a study as you possibly can.

Some of the questions I have found to be the most useful include:

1. What do you see as the most important technical developments or improvements in the last three years?
2. Which firms in the industry have done the most to increase productivity? How have they done it?
3. Which firms in the industry have done the best job of increasing sales? How have they done it?
4. What are the most significant opportunities for profit in the industry over the next five years?
5. What will be the biggest roadblocks to progress in the industry over the next five years?

6. Who are the five or six industry leaders I should be talking to if I want to get a good insight into the state of the industry?
7. Would you buy a business in this industry at this time? Why?

As you read through these questions and those in the Appendix, I'm sure others will emerge. I would try to keep the list to no more than ten or twelve good questions.

After trade journals and newsletters, trade associations are an excellent source of information. Frequently, you will find that the trade journal for an industry is published by the trade association. You want to talk to the senior executives at the association. You want to find out what is happening within the industry. Where is it going? Is it consolidated or fragmented? What kind of publications and directories does the association publish? Most trade associations publish an annual directory of members and suppliers. Many of the industry and trade associations do elaborate censuses and other statistical studies of their industry. You want to get as much of this information as you can in order to help you in your selection.

Finally, there are the financial publications such as *Forbes*, *Fortune*, *Business Week*, *Inc.*, *Venture* and the *Wall Street Journal*. There is also *U.S. Industrial Outlook*, published by the Department of Commerce for 145 major industries each year. You should read their articles on the industry you have selected and compare their projections.

- You want an industry with an uptrend. You want an industry that will show growth over the next five years.
- You are looking for an industry that is established.
- You are looking for an industry that is fragmented, with the companies tending to be smaller and medium-size firms.
- You are looking for an industry in which your experience, expertise and knowledge will help you in acquiring your LBO.

Before you begin your search, you've got to decide what kind of business you're looking for; so you must ask yourself some questions about your personal ambitions.

- Are you looking for a manufacturing firm or do you want to be in the distribution business?
- Are you looking for a retail operation or a service business?
- Where do you want the business to be located?
- How big should it be? I have said that you should be looking for businesses in the $500,000 to $10 million range of annual sales. My own experience is that the best deals for the first-time buyer are in the $2 to $5 million range.
- Do you want to be an absentee owner, or do you want to be the daily manager of the business?
- What level of risk are you willing to accept?
- Are you looking for a business that is very highly leveraged, or are you willing to put a little of your own money into the situation in order to reduce the risk level and amount of leverage that is involved?
- Even if you do not have any of your own money to put into the deal, are you willing to share equity?
- Would you accept an active or passive partner who owned even a small part of your business?

You must also ask yourself if you are willing to spend the six to twelve months it may take to find your first LBO. Remember that, typically, you will look at a dozen deals before you find one that you can actually buy. Then you may spend up to 400 hours on the deal that you actually do. You may have to spend a lot of those hours discarding the bad ones until you get to the one that you actually do. You may not be able to devote full time to this effort. It may not be possible to leave your present job or profession.

You must have your own personal objectives and criteria clearly developed, so that you do not waste your time.

A real buyer, one who is actually capable of closing a deal, has several personal characteristics that are essential to successful deal making. The main quality is a strong desire to own all, or a substantial portion, of a business. And the distinguishing characteristic of a real buyer is persistence. You must be able to go through each and every one of those 400 hours. You must be able to go back time after time until you have looked at each and every one of those dozen businesses. You cannot cut corners when trying to do a deal simply because you are bored or tired with the process. That is how you make mistakes. This is a very easy area in which to do bad deals and a very dificult on in which to do the one good deal you want. Patience, a good sense of timing and a highly disciplined approach to the allocation and use of your time are other traits you will find very useful in becoming a real buyer. You must be patient; you must wait for the right opportunity before you move. You must know when to move—and this is where the sense of timing comes in—and you must use your time in a disciplined way so that you are not wasting it chasing the wrong deal. The "wanna-be" buyers have the desire, but, frankly, they lack the guts to take action and handle the risk involved in doing real deals.

Think Like a Hunter

If you are still with me, you have decided that you are a real buyer. Now we are going to begin our search for a real seller. You have a written list of your acquisition criteria. You have selected your target industry. Now you are ready to go prospecting for your first LBO.

To succeed in finding your first LBO, you are going to have to think like a hunter, not like a trapper. You have to go out and actively pursue your LBO candidates. Do not wait for your opportunities to come to you.

How do you begin? You are going to take your acquisition criteria and turn them into three things:

- classified advertising copy
- a letter
- a telephone script

You should actively pursue all three channels. You should use three different approaches at the same time in finding your candidates.

Where are you going to put the ads? Remember those trade journals and newsletters you called when you were selecting the right industry? You are going back into those same publications and run classified ads like the others you find in those publications. You should read several of them to get an idea of the kind of wording that you feel will work for you. Your ad should state your acquisition criteria and sound, as much as possible, like you talking. After all, you are doing the looking.

The ad should be simple and direct. Do not make the language complicated. State what it is you are looking for, such as: "I want to buy your manufacturing business with sales of $2 to $5 million, must be cash positive and show a profit for the last three years." Do not get fancy. You are trying to make a connection here with a candidate.

Use a blind box number for your responses. Do not list your name and home or business address. You will be inundated with responses. You will have people knocking down the doors, calling you at all hours trying to unload their bad businesses on you. That is not what you want. You are the hunter—you want to do the selecting. Most trade journals and business newspapers such as the *Wall Street Journal* have blind box facilities. They will collect the mail and forward it to you.

Remember, the issue from the seller's point of view is confidentiality. He is not going to want to let his customers, suppliers and employees know that his business is for sale. It is easier for a potential seller to respond in confidence to your box number if you are very clear about what you are looking for and are not merely on a general fishing expedition.

Although some industries are exceptions, as a general rule, there is no time of the month or year better than another to run an acquisition search ad in a trade journal. If you have decided to go the *Wall Street Journal* route, I suggest that you run your ad in the business opportunity section on Thursday. That is traditionally the day on which you are likely to get the biggest response to your request. The main problem you are going to have is sorting through the responses in order to come up with the ones that you actually want to contact to set up a first meeting.

What about responding to sellers' ads? Sellers do run ads. As you go through trade journals, industry newsletters and the Thursday edition of the *Wall Street Journal* in the classified section under "Business Opportunities," you will notice a number of businesses for sale. You will notice that many of the businesses for sale are being offered by intermediaries—merger and acquisition firms or Biz Op brokers. Many of these companies will be running into the problems mentioned earlier in terms of confidentiality. They will tend to be the companies that are not good LBO candidates because either their growth has been so strong that they can command all cash deals or their balance sheet is going to be very weak. The former are very exciting acquisition candidates and will not be interested in a leveraged buyer. The latter are so risky that they are not viable business propositions at any price under any terms. Remember, you do not want to do a deal simply because it is available. You want the right deal.

In answering sellers' ads you should distinguish between those ads being run by brokers, which you should ignore, and the ads that are run by the companies themselves. These companies are going to find themselves inundated by many amateur buyers. It is going to be difficult for the sellers to sort through the various contacts they will receive. In self-defense, they are very likely to develop strict qualification criteria—such as, "Send us your business plan, your credentials and your financial statements" —just to weed out the amateurs before they will even consent to a first meeting. Since it is your role as a hunter to define not only what it is that you are looking for but also how you will approach the LBO candidate, the chances are slim that you will find the kind of company that you are looking for in responding to ads that sellers run.

In my experience, the best LBO candidate frequently may not even be sure that he actually wants to sell his business. He does not have anything more than an itch, a suspicion, a slight nagging doubt that he would rather be somewhere else doing something else. This does not apply to the situation of a forced sale as a result of death, divorce or partnership dissolution. But in most cases where you have a single proprietor who owns the thing completely, the founding entrepreneur has only vague feelings before he makes the conscious decision to actually sell his business. Your approach may be the first time that he has faced the complex issues involved in selling.

The Letter

I have said that you were going to turn that acquisition criteria list into a letter. To whom are you going to send that letter? In the library, especially if you have a good business school, college or university library nearby, you are going to find numerous directories of industrial firms, distributorships and retail and service organizations. Dun & Bradstreet, Standard & Poor and Thomas publish them nationally. There are many others that are published on a local or regional basis. In the directories you will find companies organized by volume of sales, by geography and by Standard Industrial Classification code, which tells you what kind of business it is. For every industry and industry segment in the country there is an SIC code.

The directory listing, typically, will include the name of the company; its dollar volume of sales; its address and telephone number; whether it is a corporation, partnership or proprietorship; and the names of the key individuals, officers, directors and other key employees. It will usually describe the product line or lines the company makes or sells, give some indication of how old the business is and indicate whether or not it has operating subsidiaries, relationships with other firms, or other locations from which it does business. This is all very useful information to have. From the list that you develop out of these directories you will begin to call the suspects that meet your acquisition criteria. You will also send letters to the chairman of the board and the president or chief executive officer. Keep your approach simple, stating who you are and what it is that you are looking for in clear, uncomplicated language. The direct approach in acquisition search is always the best. In addition to contacting the companies directly to tell them that you are looking for a business with specific characteristics, you should also ask if they know of businesses that meet your profile and if they would have them contact you. This gets the ball rolling.

SAMPLE PROSPECT LETTER

Mr. Sam F. Sulik, President
Samco, Inc.
Industrial Parkway
Cleveland, Ohio

Dear Mr. Sulik:

You have been mentioned to me by several leading suppliers in the industry as one of the most knowledgeable company presidents in the area.

I am looking for a good, solid business in the industry to acquire for my own investment. The firm I am looking for should have annual sales in the $2 to $5 million range. It should be profitable and well managed. I prefer a firm with clear, well-defined market niches and a strong reputation for quality and customer service.

If you know of a local business that meets my criteria, would you please contact me by phone or letter at the above address.

Thank you for your assistance in this matter.

Sincerely,
Lionel Haines

You may want to approach merger and acquisition intermediaries with the same letter letting them know that you are in the market and setting forth your acquisition criteria. You have a problem with the M & A intermediaries in that not all of them are familiar with or have experience in dealing with the leveraged buyout buyer. Many of them come from the all-cash school of thinking. They are not going to be receptive to a buyer who comes to them with a leveraged buyout approach to companies on which they have listings. There are two reasons for this. First, they do not know how to structure leveraged buyout deals. Second, in an LBO, they can't see where their brokerage fees are going to come from.

Phone Calls

Phone calls will probably be your most productive source of leads. Who are you going to call? Primarily, you are going to call industry suppliers. You will also be going back to the trade journal publishers, editors, ad managers and senior editors you contacted earlier. You are also going to recontact the trade association executives. Identify yourself and tell them that you would like to acquire a company in their industry. Repeat your criteria on size, type, location and other characteristics. Work from a script. In each case you will be seeking the same information and you do not want to leave out some important factor. This can save you hundreds of hours of not having to analyze companies that do not meet your acquisition criteria.

SAMPLE TELEPHONE SCRIPT

"Hello, Mr. Blank. This is Lionel Haines. I am looking for a business to buy in your industry as a personal investment. Several local suppliers have referred me to you as one of the most knowledgeable and reputable men in the industry. If you could spare me a couple of minutes of your time, I would appreciate your help."

Mr. Blank will say "Yes," "No," or "Some other time." If it is "No," go on to your next call. If it is "Some other time," set a firm time and date to follow up. If it is "Yes," read him your list of acquisition criteria and ask him if he knows of a business that meets these qualifications.

I know this may sound like a game, but you may well scare off a good prospect by saying something too direct such as, "Is your business for sale?" Because he has not confronted the issue of selling, his truthful answer will be "No." But if you let him project his own business into the picture you create with your acquisition criteria and you give him some time to think it over, he may call you back; then you suggest a meeting.

Suppliers, because they are extending credit to companies in their industry, try to know as much as they can about the condition and direction of their customers. Because not all potential LBO candidates have been able to keep the facts a complete secret, suppliers are generally your best source for finding LBO candidates. Typically, the owners will have informed one or two suppliers that they are thinking of retiring and getting out of the business.

Why would the supplier be motivated to work with you as an LBO buyer? There are two reasons. Suppliers know that liquidation is far more common than a sale. Rather than lose a good customer, they would prefer to see a good buyer come in and continue the operation of the business. The suppliers are motivated by their own self-interest to see that businesses continue in operation. If you are a credible buyer, the suppliers may even go as far as to set up appointments and provide introductions to the potential candidate.

I have found that insurance salesmen are a particularly good source of leads. Insurance salesmen are not only aggressive and out in the market, but they are also aware of the most intimate details of the financial and physical health of entrepreneurs. They know the types and amounts of insurance that entrepreneurs are buying. They frequently know of pending retirements through pension plan activities. If you find the right insurance salesman in the industry that you have targeted, work with him on a referral or finder's fee basis. Indicate to him that for every successful deal he brings you, you would be willing to give him a fee of $2,000 to $5,000, or even $10,000, depending on the size of the deal. You will find that this arrangement will be an excellent source of deal referrals.

Some other sources of referrals are bankers and other lenders, lawyers, certified public accountants and business consultants. Because they are not always "deal oriented," it is difficult to motivate them to look for a really likely LBO candidate on your behalf. This will be especially true if you are a stranger to them. Even if you deal with bankers, lawyers and CPAs you know, think a minute. How many deals have they mentioned to you in the past year? They are not really your best source. But as you set out, give them a try when you cannot get anywhere with your ads, letters and phone calls.

Finally, don't waste your time looking in the business opportunity classified ads in your daily newspapers or dealing with your local business opportunity brokers. Most Biz Op brokers are real estate brokers who have switched from selling commercial real estate to selling mom-and-pop businesses. They rarely, if ever, see a good LBO candidate in the $500,000 to $10 million range. Most of the deals they do are at or below $500,000, usually far below. The Biz Op broker gets his fees entirely up front from the cash in the deal. On an LBO he simply does not see where his fee is coming from, so he is not motivated to work with you. Furthermore, he is not willing to spend the time or energy to learn techniques or go through the lengthy negotiations that may be necessary in order to conclude a leveraged buyout.

The deals that you will see in the ads or through the Biz Op broker are going to be thoroughly shopped. They are not going to be the good, successful businesses. If you are going to do this, I want you to buy a good, successful business. Do not buy another job. It is not worth the time and energy that you are going to spend. Remember, this search could easily take you six months to a year. You could spend hundreds of hours looking at twelve to fourteen businesses before you find the one deal that you can actually do. These businesses in the ads or listed with the Biz Op brokers are the mom-and-pop businesses that are hanging on by a thread. Frequently, they are in trouble. Those are not the kind of businesses you want to buy at any price on any terms.

It is important to persevere. Your persistence will pay. It will be difficult to remember to continually keep busy, to stay involved, to remain focused on your goal. Each day you should take some step—no matter how small—toward your next goal. You will have to keep pushing yourself to find yet another candidate.

I spent over three months trying to find a firm in Southern California that specialized in recycling computer components and electronic scrap to recover the precious metals. When I began, there were 629 firms on my list. I had to call each and every firm to sort out those that actually processed their own electronic scrap from those that shipped it overseas for processing. I asked the same questions day after day, week after week, until I had eliminated all but twenty-three. From the twenty-three, I had to obtain additional information, drive by and inspect the premises, find out how large the lots were, how big the buildings were, what kind of condition they were in. The twenty-three companies that were my finalists were located in eighteen different municipal jurisdictions. Each jurisdiction had different regulations regarding scrap yards and the handling of hazardous wastes. Each one of the operating permits had to be checked out to determine whether or not the companies were operating within the law. The kind of equipment and its operating condition had to be checked. It is one thing to say in an ad that you can recover precious metals. It is an entirely different thing to actually have the crucibles, furnaces, molds and other hardware you need in order to actually recover them profitably.

Once all of this information had been obtained, there were the Dun & Bradstreet reports to check. From my list of twenty-three companies I was able to obtain Dun & Bradstreet reports on twenty-one of them. I was now nearly three months into the process and I had to further narrow the selection on the basis of size, because I was looking for a company with sales between $1 and $3 million. To come up with my list of the final three candidates took something over ninety days. When I had finished I made an appointment with a local consultant who specialized in the industry. I showed him my three prospects. He laughed and said, "You know, I wouldn't have thought of any of them, but they are the three best small companies in the local industry." I was pleased to hear that my time and effort in going through the process, making those 600-odd telephone calls and doing the rest of the legwork had actually produced good, successful LBO candidates. The point is to persevere: be persistent, be patient, continue to do the work. Even if you do just one bit a day in your search, you will have moved the process along and you will be building your confidence that you can do these deals.

I do not recommend that you begin by getting Dun & Bradstreet reports on every company that you are considering as a candidate. There are two reasons for this. One, Dun & Bradstreet reports, in terms of financial information, are frequently out of date and incomplete. After all, most of the information is provided by the company itself at the request of Dun & Bradstreet. Understandably, the companies are going to present the best picture they can of their own financial condition. Moreover, the reports are difficult to obtain if you are not a subscriber and they are expensive. I have paid anywhere from $15 to $25 for Dun & Bradstreet reports. When I do need them, I have found that working through brokers or banks is the best way to obtain them.

From these reports you can determine the names, the ages and the backgrounds of the principals involved. Dun & Bradstreet is usually fairly accurate on the breakdown of equity ownership, because that is largely a matter of public record. What you are looking for is the entrepreneur who is the sole owner, with 100 percent control. It is far easier in LBO negotiations to be involved with a single entity. Every time you add another person to the seller's team you multiply the problems greatly. It is far easier to deal with a single seller.

FINDING THE RIGHT INDUSTRY

Ten Businesses Most Likely to Survive

1. Funeral Home
2. Tobacco Wholesaler
3. Fuel Oil Dealer
4. Laundry & Dry Cleaner
5. Drugstore
6. Hotel

7. Wood Products Manufacturer
8. Personal Services
9. Beer & Wine Wholesaler
10. Service Station

SOURCE: Dun & Bradstreet/Small Business Administration

Ten Most Successful Privately Owned Businesses *

1. Hotel
2. Pharmaceuticals Manufacturer
3. Oil Production
4. Metal Products Manufacturer
5. Scientific & Photographic Equipment
6. Furniture Manufacturer
7. Glass & Concrete Manufacturer
8. Transportation Equipment Manufacturer
9. Electronics Manufacturer & Distributor
10. Equipment Rental

SOURCE: Enterprise Network
* Highest profit, best total owner's compensation and sales growth.

TEN FASTEST GROWTH INDUSTRIES
(SALES REVENUES)

Industry	SIC Code	Compound Annual Growth Rate in Constant Dollars, 1982–87
Semiconductor & Related Devices	3674	34.1%
Electronic Computing Equipment	3573	19.2%
Optical Instruments & Lenses	3832	16.7%
X-ray Apparatus & Tubes	3693	15.4%
Medicinals & Botanicals	2833	13.9%
Calculating & Accounting Machines	3574	13.0%
Biological Products	2831	12.2%
Electronic Connectors	3678	10.6%

Electrical Measuring Devices	3825	10.0%
Lithographic Platemaking		
Services	2795	9.8%

SOURCE: U.S. Department of Commerce

FINDING THE RIGHT BUSINESS

If your local library does not have these titles, contact the publisher directly.

Industry Outlook:
1985 U.S. Industrial Outlook
Five-year forecast for over 350 industries.
U.S. Department of Commerce
Bureau of Industrial Economics
Washington, DC 20402

Trade Associations:
National Trade and Professional Associations of the United States
Columbia Books, Inc.
1350 New York Ave., N.W., Suite 207
Washington, DC 20005
20th Annual Edition, 1985

Encyclopedia of Associations
Gale Research Co.
Book Tower
Detroit, MI 48226

Trade Publications:
Business Rates & Data—Part I
The standard reference. Listed by industry.
Standard Rate & Data Service, Inc.
3004 Glenview Road
Wilmette, IL 60091
1-800-323-4601

Company Directories:
Million Dollar Directory
Volume 1: Companies with a net worth of $1.2 million
   or more
Volume 2: Companies with a net worth of $900,000 to
   $1.2 million

Volume 3: Companies with a net worth of $500,000
                to $900,000
Dun & Bradstreet, Inc.
3 Century Dr.
Parsippany, NJ 07054

Thomas Register of American Manufacturers
Thomas Publishing Co.
1 Penn Plaza
New York, NY 10119

Manufacturers Register
Published on a state-to-state basis for California, Washington, Oregon, Arizona, Colorado, Utah, Idaho, Texas and Illinois.
Times Mirror Press
1115 S. Boyle Ave.
Los Angeles, CA 90023

M & A Intermediaries:
Directory of Intermediaries
The leading source of information on merger and acquisition intermediaries in the United States
Buyout Publications
7124 Convoy Ct.
San Diego, CA 92111

3

How to Tell If It's Right

There is a saying among LBO deal makers that you make your money on the deals that you do not do, on the ones you are smart enough to walk away from, on the ones that look almost good enough but that little "something" just is not right. We are going to explore how you can tell if a deal really is the right deal for you. We are going to approach the analysis of deals. Deal analysis, or due diligence, as it is called, involves many issues, tests, ratios and criteria, but the most important one of all is the gut test. If any deal that you are looking at does not pass your gut test, if you feel uneasy about it, if the chemistry just is not right, if you suspect that the potential seller is misleading you, not telling you the whole story, walk away. There are literally thousands of potential LBO candidates out there. You can find a deal you can do, a deal that you can live with, if you are simply patient and persevere. Whatever else happens in the course of deal analysis, if you find that this deal is not passing your gut test, if something is nagging you, telling you that it is not right—drop it. Walk away. Because you make your money on the deals you do not do.

Due diligence is the cautious, concerned, intelligent analysis that you would put into making any investment by becoming aware of all of the risks and opportunities. Due diligence is the process by which you familiarize yourself with the parameters of an investment you are considering.

You should approach each deal very carefully. Keep your eyes wide open, ask hard questions and keep on asking hard questions until you get hard answers.

In this chapter, I will show you how to analyze a business as an LBO candidate and how to tell if it is the right deal for you. A complete checklist of due diligence questions, the hard questions that rarely get asked, will be found in the Appendix at the end of the book. I am also going to take a rather lengthy look at how to read financial statements, particularly the balance sheet and the income statement, or P & L. There are two reasons for this. First, you must be familiar with the organization and content of financial statements so that you will be able to tell at a glance whether any particular candidate has real LBO potential. Second, I want to show you how to reschedule or recast the balance sheet and the income statement, as if you were the owner of the candidate business, to see how your leveraged buyout would impact the business. This will help you to determine the feasibility of doing a particular deal.

A good business is like a good milking stool. It stands on three legs. Whatever the business, there is a sales and marketing component—you have to sell something. Whatever the business, it offers goods or services—there's a production or operational aspect. That is the second leg. And somebody has to count the money, keep track of the paper clips, hire and fire and take care of the general administrative and financial aspects of the business. This is the last leg of the milking stool. All three of these areas—marketing, operations and administration—are critical in your due diligence. A quick review of the due diligence questions in the Appendix will introduce you to some of the key issues in each of these three areas. The questions will give you some guidelines and criteria for deal analysis so that you can come up with the hard answers you need to get comfortable with a potential deal.

A word about attorneys and CPAs. While they may not be the best source of leads to LBO candidates, do not think about approaching a leveraged buyout transaction without a good deal-oriented attorney and a good deal-oriented CPA on your side. There is nothing more expensive than cheap help. There is nothing cheaper than expensive help. Do not try to save money by going after a cut-rate lawyer or accountant in your deal. It is in the nature of entrepreneurs that they like to be their own brain surgeons. They want to do it all themselves. Do not fall into that trap. It is not necessary for you to bring your attorney and CPA in on each and every one of the parts of your deal, but when you get to due diligence, you are going to want to have your attorney and CPA involved.

One of the mistakes that first-time LBO buyers make is that the very excitement of the process gets them going so much that they are tempted to take shortcuts in due diligence just to get the deal done. This usually happens with the first or second deal they look at. It looks so good, and they have already put so much time into studying this material, finding the right industry and getting prepared, that they are afraid the deal is going to get away from them. In the heat of the moment they take shortcuts in their due diligence just to get the deal done. You may feel that the hard questions and intense investigation necessary to do a good, thorough job of due diligence may offend the seller, but remember, he is selling you his business. Make him sell it to you. It is up to him to fully inform you of all of the areas of your concern. After all, a successful business transaction is a win-win proposition. If you do not fully satisfy the needs and concerns of the seller, then he is not going to sell you his business. By the same token, if your criteria and personal objectives are not met, if all of your needs and concerns are not dealt with, then you will not be a winner. Then you may end up owning a business that you do not want or do not like, and that you may not be able to run. Do not be ashamed or embarrassed. Do not be afraid to ask the hard questions. Do not be embarrassed to conduct an intense investigation. You will not offend a serious seller by showing him that you are a serious buyer—one who is going to explore fully and completely the risks and opportunities offered by his business. Do not sacrifice your standards or your acquisition criteria in order to simply do a deal. If you have developed sound criteria that reflect your real needs and thought them through in the beginning, then stick with them. Do not lower your standards just to get a deal done that looks very good on the surface. It really is not worth it. Remember, you make your money here on the deals you do not do.

Financial statements, or financials, are the various accounting reports that present a picture of the financial condition of a company. The most common financial statements are the balance sheet and the income statement or profit and loss (P & L) statement. Other common financials, especially if the statements have been prepared by or compiled by an accountant, cover shareholders' equity, changes in financial condition and cash flow.

You can learn something from all of them, but realistically, in most of the deals you will consider, the seller will have only a balance sheet and a P & L. So we will focus on them. The balance sheet is a numbers snapshot of a company at a point in time that sets forth that which the company owns—its assets—and that which the company owes—its liabilities. The amount of assets less liabilities is called owner's equity or shareholders' equity or book value or net worth.

If you are unfamiliar with basic business accounting, or even a little rusty, this would be a good point for a quick review. It is not my purpose to make a bookkeeper or accountant out of you, but you must know what to look for when you look at a potential seller's financials.

A Painless Way to Read Financial Statements

Getting down to the real nitty gritty of whether or not you have found a good deal you can do begins and ends with the financial statements.

You are going to need financial statements for the last three years. If you have them for more than three years, say five or even ten years, fine, but they really don't mean much. The statute of limitations on fraud only runs back three years, so any representation the potential seller makes in his financial statements is only valid for three years from your point of view.

The financial statements—the actual documents themselves—are going to tell you something about a business. For example, the amount of detail in the financial statements can be revealing. Normally, a set of financials is organized with the balance sheet as the first page, then the P & L, then the statement of changes in financial condition or sources and uses of cash. If they are included, other statements and the footnotes are added as the last page or two in the set.

• Begin by examining the balance sheet. Is this a highly detailed financial statement? For example, under cash do you find such items listed as "cash in First National Bank," "cash in Second National Bank," "cash in cash register," "cash in petty cash drawer." and so on? Usually, this kind of detail is a sign that you are dealing with a really inexperienced or amateur entrepreneur, one who is not financially sophisticated. He may even be doing his own books and records. These are not the kind of polished financial statements that have been prepared with the help of an accountant. If they have been prepared by an independent CPA, you will find a letter stating the terms and conditions under which the accountant prepared the statements and disclaiming any responsibility if anything less than a full audit was undertaken. Very rarely will you find yourself looking at audited financial statements for businesses in the $500,000 to $10 million range. This should not throw you. It is not a deal breaker. It is simply the way of the world in businesses of this size. Footnotes, if they have been included, can be the source of much useful information, but normally you will not have them to work with. You will have only a balance sheet and an income statement.

• You should ask the potential seller whether he has had a tax audit. Chances are that he will not have had one. The main reason you want to do this is to establish the fact that the books and records have not been audited and that there is no IRS tax audit. These are primarily negotiating points for further on in the process. They have nothing to do with your analysis of the deal.

• You are going to look at assets on the balance sheet to find the source of the down payment for the deal. You are going to look at the income statement (P & L) to determine if there is enough cash available to service any debt you might use in financing the deal. Typically, LBO deals are structured on the basis of 25 percent cash down and 75 percent financing. Look to the balance sheet for the down payment and to the income statement for debt service.

The Balance Sheet

The balance sheet begins with assets (that which the company owns) followed by liabilities (that which the company owes). The difference between the two is net worth or book value or shareholders' equity. Assets are normally found on the top of the balance sheet or on the left-hand side; liabilities and net worth are usually presented on the bottom or on the right-hand side of the balance sheet. The example of Sam's balance sheet from Samco, Inc. will give you the general idea.

Balance sheets are further organized into the categories of current and long-term or fixed. You will find assets and liabilities ranked by their liquidity (or their nearness to cash). Those assets that are called current are assets that are cash or can be turned into cash within twelve months. Long-term or fixed assets are those that could only be turned into cash in more than twelve months. The same holds true for liabilities. There are current liabilities, which are debts or bills that are due to be paid within twelve

SAMCO BALANCE SHEET

June 30, 198_

ASSETS

Cash	$ 40,000	
Accounts Receivable	$428,000	
Notes Receivable	$ 38,000	
Inventory	$235,000	
TOTAL CURRENT ASSETS		$741,000

FIXED ASSETS

Furniture & Fixtures	$ 22,000	
Equipment & Machinery	$223,000	
Vehicles	$ 41,000	
TOTAL FIXED ASSETS		$286,000
OTHER ASSETS		$ 17,000
TOTAL ASSETS		**$1,044,000**

LIABILITIES

Accounts Payable	$109,000	
Short-Term Notes	$ 39,000	
Deposits on Contracts	$346,000	
Taxes Payable	$ 17,000	
TOTAL CURRENT LIABILITIES		$511,000

LONG-TERM LIABILITIES

Notes Payable	$ 38,000	
TOTAL LONG-TERM LIABILITIES		$ 38,000
TOTAL LIABILITIES		$ 549,000

NET WORTH

Shareholders' Equity		$ 495,000
TOTAL LIABILITIES & NET WORTH		**$1,044,000**

months; then there are the long-term liabilities, which are due in the time beyond twelve months.

What you are looking for on the balance sheet are hard assets—assets that are easy to value, that can be readily liquidated and on which there is no debt. An ideal LBO balance sheet would show:

- very few current liabilities
- almost no long-term liabilities
- a high book value or net worth

You are also going to look at the quality of earnings. Profits or retained earnings show up in the balance sheet in a number of ways. Profits can show up as cash or as accounts receivable; they can show up in fixtures and equipment. What you are looking for are earnings that show up in cash or accounts receivable. The further away from cash the earnings show up in the balance sheet, the weaker the business.

What do I mean by that? Take the example of a company that provides scientific equipment to a major corporation such as IBM. Under the terms of the contract, the company you are considering is required to undertake a certain amount of research and development. That requires it to buy new equipment and fixtures every two or three years. Some of the earnings from the contract with IBM will show up as fixed assets (the new equipment), not in cash or accounts receivable. This is a difference in the quality of earnings—the company may be showing a very high profit margin, but the quality of the earnings is not as good as in another company whose profits show up on its balance sheet in accounts receivable or cash. You are looking for hard assets and you are looking for a high quality of earnings in that balance sheet.

Cash   Go to the example of Samco, Inc.'s balance sheet and start at the top with cash. If you are looking for assets, cash is a very good asset, but why would a seller sell you his cash? Remember the capital gains tax rate? If Sam takes the cash out of his business, it will be taxed as income before it leaves the company and as dividend income to Sam. But if he sells you his cash as an asset of the business, then the cash is subject to capital gains treatment. In this approach, Sam is going to realize more net cash in the sale. That is why Sam is going to sell you his cash.

Accounts Receivable Right around the corner from cash, we have accounts receivable. They are the number-one asset with the asset-based lenders who could be involved in financing your leveraged buyout. Accounts receivable are the money that is owed to the company for goods or services it provided to its customers. I am assuming that the accounts receivable are viable. In other words, these accounts are less than ninety days old and the goods have been delivered or the services have been performed. This has to be determined from the accounts receivable aging analysis you get from the seller. When you go over the accounts receivable aging analysis you are going to look to see if there is any one dominant customer and you are going to look to see how the customers have been paying their bills. You should look for any customers who have been dragging their payments out and exceeding the amount allocated for bad debts or write-offs, which is usually 1.5 to 3 percent of the total amount due.

When an asset-based lender is going through the process of verifying and evaluating your accounts receivable, the first question he will ask the accountant is "Have the goods actually been delivered or have the services actually been performed?" If the business has a valid account and it is not more than ninety days old, the lender is going to accept it as collateral for financing.

The same principle applies to notes receivable, although they are not as near to cash. When you find notes receivable on the balance sheets of small businesses it is frequently because loans were made to employees or officers and directors of the company. They are not producing assets of the business in the sense that they are not needed for its operation.

Inventory Inventory means many things, depending on whether you are looking at a manufacturing business, a distribution business or a retail store. Service businesses rarely, if ever, have much inventory beyond office supplies and promotional materials. Inventory is almost always the most controversial asset on the balance sheet in an LBO. The seller, in his attempt to shelter his income from the Internal Revenue Service, will have done wonderful things with his inventory. If he is a manufacturer, he will have expensed off tens of thousands, perhaps hundreds of thousands, of dollars of inventory. I have seen a precious-metals processing company that was able to carry gold at $35 and $40 an ounce on its books in a market where gold was selling for $330 to $350 an ounce. The owner did this in order to avoid taxes. But since he didn't have an exit plan, he didn't know how to get the real value out of the company and not get hit with a big tax penalty. The difference between the stated book value of the inventory and its real market value is the place where hidden assets can be found. This is to your advantage as the buyer, because you can leverage those assets. Do not get into an argument with the seller over their actual worth. Simply acknowledge the fact that they exist and smile, because he has just made your job a little easier.

There are at least four approaches to dealing with inventory in structuring a deal, and when I get to deal structuring I will go into them in some detail. On first analysis, you are looking for the amount of inventory as it actually exists, not as it is stated on the balance sheet. Inventory is not as highly valued as accounts receivable for collateral by asset-based lenders because of its liquidity and the more volatile changes in value to which it is subject. You can benefit from doing an aging analysis of the inventory. You will want to determine the total dollar value of inventory for each of the following categories: that which has been around for less than six months; six months to one year; one year to eighteen months; and finally, the inventory that has been around for over eighteen months. Generally speaking, the older the inventory, the less value it has. This aging analysis will give you an idea of how the inventory has been moving through the company.

Fixed Assets Fixed assets are the assets that are slower to liquidate and cannot readily be turned into cash. Typical fixed assets are the fixtures and furniture, machinery and equipment, vehicles and real estate.

Every asset has three values.

• The going business value is the actual value of the thing itself, plus the cost of labor and materials required for its installation. That is what is carried on the books as going business value.

• The orderly liquidation value is the value of the asset less the cost of labor and materials for installation. If I sell the asset to you, you are going to have to pay to have it disconnected, moved and reassembled or reconnected in your facility. You do not want to pay me for my cost of installation because it has no value to you and your cost of installation and transportation is going to be added to your cost.

• The scrap or salvage value, also known as the fire sale value, the under-the-hammer value and other equally colorful and descriptive terms. This is what you could get if you had to move the asset out the door in a few days.

These are the three theoretical values. From the standpoint of doing an LBO, however, there are really only two values to every asset. The most important to you is what kind of a return the asset produces for the business. Because if an asset does not produce a profit for the business it is not an asset. Remember, your return is profit. Profit is expressed in terms of return on investment, return on equity or return on assets. So the only real value of an asset is what kind of a profit it is returning to the business. The other value of an asset is its appraised value as collateral to the asset-based lender who will be financing the deal. This is a short-term, more immediate concern, but it is a concern of real value. If you cannot get American Appraisal or one of the other independent, third-party appraisers to give an estimate of value on an asset, then you cannot plan on using that asset as a part of the collateral for your financing. So, forget the three theoretical values of an asset and focus on the two real values: what kind of a profit it will return for the business, and how much money you can sell it for or borrow against it as you are looking for financing of your LBO.

On some balance sheets you will see a category labeled "Other Assets." These are the assets that no one expects will ever be turned into cash, but the Internal Revenue Service required the entrepreneur to carry them as assets and depreciate them rather than write them off as expenses. The most common is good will, which is the main nondepreciable asset. But there are some others such as start-up costs, brochures, deposits and prepaid expenses, patents, copyrights and research and development expenses. There is very, very little hope that any of these sunk costs will ever turn into cash. They should not enter into your calculations when you are looking for hard assets as the basis for financing your LBO.

You are looking for hidden assets. That is why you keep asking questions of the seller. In negotiating (Chapter 7), there are many questions I will suggest you ask during your first visit. Because in addition to such things as inventory and equipment that are carried on the books at one value but may really be worth a considerable amount more, there are such hidden assets as the cash value of life insurance policies. These are never carried on the books but do exist and can be turned into cash in order to help make a down payment.

I have said that you do not want to get into an argument with the seller on his statements as to the real value of his assets. When he tells you that his custom-made punch press or lathe or his delivery truck is actually worth a whole lot more than is shown on the books, just agree with him and make a note. Because in a leveraged buyout, when you are going to be determining the value of the company in order to set a purchase price, you are going to be paying the owner dollar for dollar on the value of his assets but you will be paying him a multiple on his earnings. The thing to remember here about assets is depreciation. If a company has $100,000 worth of fixed assets and is writing them off over a five-year period, that is $20,000 a year in depreciation that is deducted as an operating expense right out of pretax profit. If the seller tells you that the fixed assets are really worth $500,000 and you start arguing with him, look at what you are doing. That $500,000 worth of fixed assets written off over five years means $100,000 a year in depreciation that comes right off the bottom line. That is why you can afford to pay him dollar for dollar for his assets. Whatever he says they are worth you accept because he is lowering the price of the company by diminishing the profit, because you are going to pay him a multiple of three, four or five times his earnings in order to arrive at a price for the company. So never dispute the seller if he tells you that his fixed assets are worth more than they are shown on the books.

How much is the machinery and equipment worth? You must determine if it can pay for itself in eighteen months. In other words, can the profit it generates pay the price and return the original investment to you completely in eighteen months? One way to look at this is to find out what is the top price you could pay on used machinery and equipment. It will be some percentage of the price you could pay for brand-new, state-of-the-art equipment or machinery. For example, if a new lathe costs $100,000 and produces 100 units an hour, and the lathe that you are looking at in the seller's fixed assets only produces 50 units an hour, then it can only be worth half as much because it is only half as productive. It does not make any difference what he says it is worth or what he paid for it or at what value he is carrying it on his books. Realistically, that is what you can afford to pay for it. You have to determine whether or not, taking into consideration the investment you have made plus the labor and materials needed to produce those 50 units, the profit margin is sufficient to return your entire investment in that lathe in eighteen months. If it is, then it is a piece of equipment that you will want to keep. If not, it is something you may want to think of liquidating or scrapping as soon as you take over and begin to operate the company. You can see that the leveraged buyout is most appropriate where machinery and equiment have long, useful economic lives and are not encumbered by debt.

Liabilities Turn now to the liability side of the balance sheet. Begin by looking at the accounts payable and notes payable. Accounts payable will be trade suppliers and will show the amounts owed to them for goods and services received. Notes payable can be short-term borrowings, usually bank debt or private debt. It could be money that the owner has lent the company in the form of deferred salary in order to draw it out at some future point in time as debt repayment and not as income or dividends.

There are two issues to consider with accounts payable. One is the total amount and terms, the other is the list of names and amounts due specific suppliers. You will not be able to get the list from the balance sheet, so you are going to need an accounts payable aging analysis from the seller. With the accounts payable aging analysis, what you are looking for is the role of a key or dominant supplier. Is there anyone there who is a sole source supplier? This is a key issue in determining the feasibility of operating the business. You do not want to get into a situation where your lifeline is a key supplier who is the sole source of a needed item or a vital service. You want to make sure that key suppliers are not also close friends of the seller or his family members. Those can be problematic relationships.

On accrued liabilities, the last of the items listed under current liabilities, you will find such items as unpaid vacation and sick pay, unpaid sales taxes or withholding taxes and unfunded pension plans. These entries can be a red flag. This is why you want to see at least three years' worth of financial statements, to see whether there has been any buildup in any of these accounts. It is not unusual to find a business in trouble where the entrepreneur has been using his tax money as working capital. So when you find accrued liabilities for taxes or vacation and sick pay going up at a rapid rate over the last three years, you know that you are looking at a shaky business—one that you want to avoid.

With the long-term liabilities, you will be primarily concerned with the rate of interest and the remaining term. Normally you will be looking at one or more loans made for one- to seven-year terms with interest pegged at one to five points over prime. You should ask:

- Who is the lender and what are the provisions of that loan for a change of ownership?
- Is there any assumability in the long-term debt, or is a change in ownership going to trigger off a requirement that the outstanding balance be paid in full on demand?

These are key issues.

Finally, you are going to look over the footnotes, if any. If there are none, you are going to make notes to yourself to ask the seller, about off–balance sheet or unrecorded liabilities: those that do not show up on a balance sheet. Pending lawsuits, current litigation, warranties on contracts, sales allowances or credits to customers, other leases or contractual commitments to employees or consultants are all liabilities of the company that do not necessarily show up on the balance sheet. For example, in Southern California right now, there is a fairly substantial off–balance sheet liability in many companies that are going to be required to bring their facilities up to earthquake code. This is why you will want to have a good deal-oriented attorney and CPA involved in this due diligence review with you.

In summary, when analyzing the balance sheet look for lots of financeable hard assets. There are a lot of financial ratios that can be used to analyze financials, but the one I want you to focus on is the current ratio. It is found by taking the current assets and dividing them by the current liabilities. The current ratio should be positive. A 3-to-1 ratio is good, 2 to 1 is OK. Lower than that is not going to be acceptable in most cases. If you do a current ratio analysis of the balance sheet for the last three years and you see a declining current ratio in a company with static sales, that is usually the indicator of a major problem. And that is the time you want to walk away.

BALANCE SHEET CHECKLIST

Good Signs

- High net worth (assets minus liabilities equal net worth).
- Plenty of hard, fixed assets (equipment, machinery, vehicles, real estate, etc.).
- Most of the liabilities are current bills and not long-term debt.

- Profits (also called retained earnings) show up as cash or accounts receivable.
- Inventory is mostly raw materials or finished goods and not work in progress.
- The accrued liability for taxes, pension plan payments or unused sick leave and vacation pay is small and has remained steady over the past two or three years.
- Long-term debt is assumable without personal guarantees if the business is sold.
- There are no off–balance sheet liabilities or contingent liabilities.
- The current ratio (current assets divided by current liabilities) is 2 to 1 or larger.

Bad Signs

- Negative or declining net worth (business is losing money).
- Few fixed assets, mostly office equipment and supplies. Look for leased equipment and vehicles.
- Lots of long-term debt and mortgages.
- Profits (retained earnings) do not show up on the balance sheet because owner is drawing them out as they are made.
- Inventory is old, slow-moving or mostly work in progress.
- High or rapidly growing accrued liability for taxes, pension plans and unused sick leave/vacation pay.
- There are undisclosed liabilities or pending lawsuits.

The Income Statement

We are going to turn now to consideration of the income statement. If the balance sheet is a numbers snapshot of the company at a point in time, the income statement is a summary of what the company has done over a period of time, usually a month, a quarter or a year. Unlike the famous bottom line, we are going to start with the top line, which is sales or gross revenues. These are not the same thing, as you will see.

SAMCO INCOME STATEMENT

Year Ended Dec. 31, 198_

Sales Revenues	**$3,134,000**
less Cost of Goods Sold	
Materials	843,000
Direct Labor	914,000
Gross Profit	**$1,377,000**
less Operating Expenses	
Salaries	$ 317,000
Advertising	24,000
Automobile	28,000
Depreciation	148,000
Equipment Rental	5,800
Fees & Services	5,200
Insurance	109,000
Interest	5,300
Postage & Freight	23,000
Rent	119,000
Repairs	83,000
Supplies	10,000
Taxes	129,800
Telephone & Utilities	41,000
Travel & Entertainment	22,900
Miscellaneous	28,000
Bad Debts	7,500
Net Profit	**$ 270,500**

From gross revenues we are going to take expenses to get to the bottom line, or pretax net profit. The first deduction from sales or gross revenues is normally the cost of goods sold or, as it is sometimes called, the cost of sales. Typically, that term refers to the direct labor and materials costs of the product. When you subtract the cost of goods sold from sales, you end up with a figure that is called gross profit. The gross profit margin is the gross profit expressed as a percentage of sales. This margin will vary depending on the type of business you are examining. For example, in a manufacturing business the minimum gross profit margin you will be looking for is 40 percent. In a distribution business, however, a gross profit margin of 20 percent is totally acceptable. In retailing, you will find that the gross profit margin will vary greatly depending on the volume of sales of the business. For example, a supermarket can make a good profit on a 1.5 percent margin because of the very high volume of sales. A specialty boutique may have to have a 40 percent to 50 percent margin to make a good profit because of the smaller number of sales it can make during the same period. In service businesses gross profit is a less applicable concept, but typically you would look for a 10 percent to 15 percent margin, because labor is the main expense in the cost of sales. This is the kind of information you get from trade associations, trade journals and Dun & Bradstreet.

After sales, you may see "Other Revenues." Other revenues can be interest on loans, dividends from stocks owned, income from the sale of assets, rent or incidental consulting activities. You should ignore this entry. It tells you next to nothing about the solidity of the business. The principal business of the company is its sales. That is what you will be looking at to determine if you have enough top line income to get to the bottom line with enough pretax profit to handle the debt service to finance the business. You want to know what the other revenues are and where they come from. If it is not obvious from the income statement, you should ask a follow-up question of the seller, but for determining the feasibility of doing the deal, ignore other revenue sources.

As you go down the list of expense items in the Samco income statement, I want you to keep in mind the differences between a publicly held corporation and a privately owned one. In a public corporation the whole point of the game is to maximize profit. The higher the profit, the higher the expected price/earnings ratio, which pushes up the price of the stock. The executives of a public corporation are managing their corporation in order to maximize the market price of their stock. The owner of a privately held company has an entirely different game plan. He is attempting to minimize profit so he does not have to give it to the IRS and the state. When you get into reading privately held company income statements you are going to enter the realm of creative fiction. Sometimes they are so creative that they will make you doubt the seller's honesty, but you must go through them objectively. The purpose is not to get into an argument with a potential seller but to see how he was running his business. You should look at the income statement with an eye toward how you would do things if you were in control, and that is called rescheduling or recasting. First, you are going to look at the income statement as it is to see how the seller has been running the business. Then you look at it through your eyes as if you were running the business and decide how you would change it. Finally, you write down, or recast, those figures. You are looking for dollars on your recast financial statements, because in a typical LBO deal you are going to pay 25 percent of the purchase price in a cash down payment. This cash is going to be created, in one of several ways I'll cover later, out of the assets on the balance sheet. The remaining 75 percent of the purchase price is some combination of debt and continued perks. What you want to know is whether the company can pay the debt service. It is likely that you will be able to pay all of the debt in a reasonable period of time. By that I mean three to seven years. Most typically it will be five years. However, you probably will not find sufficient working capital to also

grow the business. That is why I have continually empha-
sized the importance of buying a good, strong, successful
business in the first place. There are some low-cost techniques of growing a business but if you are looking for a big
chunk of the cash flow to help you grow that business, it is
unlikely that you will find it if you are also financing 75
percent of the purchase price out of that same cash flow. If
you do plan to grow the business, you will have to find
additional sources of cash.

Rescheduling the Income Statement

Salaries   Salaries is a category where Sam admits he is taking home $200,000 a year. Look for excessive salaries or
salaries for such phantom employees as sons, daughters,
wives, nieces, nephews and other relatives, or people who
may not even be in the company. It is not unusual to find
an entrepreneur who is putting a kid or two through college
by carrying them on the payroll as if they were employees.
These are phantom employees. You are going to have to
ask hard questions in order to get this information, but if
the seller is a real seller and is working with you to sell you
his business, you will be able to get it. In your recasting,
salaries is typically one of the items where you would look
for a reduction.

Advertising   Advertising is one of those activities that most
entrepreneurs do very poorly, if at all. It is not unusual to
find entrepreneurial advertising budgets of something like
$160, which consists of a couple of small ads in the local
school newspaper and the church bulletin. Remember, the
typical LBO candidate has mentally retired from his business several years ago. He no longer has the aggressive
urge or the financial incentive to keep his business growing,
and advertising is one of those areas in which he cuts back.
When you take over you may want to increase advertising
expenditures.

Automobile Expenses   This is an item that most entrepreneurs do not cut back. It is very difficult these days for the successful entrepreneur to get away with two Rolls-Royces and three Mercedes-Benz as he could a few years ago, because the IRS has tightened the screws a bit, but you will find some very interesting and creative perks in the automobile category. It is perfectly acceptable for you to provide yourself and your key executives with automobiles, but I think that when you look throughly at this expense you will find some more dollars for your rescheduled income statement that you can free up to help pay the debt service.

Depreciation   Depreciation dollars are not real dollars that have been spent, but they are a real deduction that reduces the bottom line. What you are looking for here is excessive depreciation allowances. If the seller has deducted too aggressively for depreciation, profits will look unrealistically low. You need to verify the basis established for depreciation. If the seller cannot tell you, certainly his bookkeeper or CPA can. You should also check the write-off period and the type of depreciation chosen with your CPA.

Equipment Rental   If you notice a figure that seems to be large, say over $10,000, you are going to want to find out if there are any equipment rental contracts. Look for a potential liability that you did not pick up when you looked at the balance sheet. These are called off-sheet liabilities. Excessive equipment rental charges may indicate an opportunity to cut expenses by buying a new piece of equipment to replace one that is rented frequently. A recent buildup in rental fees may mean maintenance problems with existing equipment.

Fees & Services   This is where you will find that the entrepreneur has not been spending much for his attorney and his accountant. Entrepreneurs are very cost-conscious. They do not like to spend money they do not have to spend. You will find them saving paper clips, turning off lights and trying to find the cheapest lawyers and bookkeepers they can. In this category for professional fees and services you would expect to find a fairly low, steady figure. Look for a pattern. It does not make too much difference how much the business has been paying for its professional services, but any abnormal highs or lows might signal an audit or litigation or some other unusual occurrence in the past three years. If you do find such variations in the pattern you are going to ask more questions. In most cases you will be increasing this figure when you are rescheduling the income statement.

Insurance Look at the insurance bills. Analyze the policies to make sure that there has been an adequate umbrella of coverage that will actually protect the business and allow it to run. Is there a new or changed product liability environment? What about environmental damage, hazardous wastes, worker's compensation and other areas to be explored. Is there officers' and directors' liability (sometimes called errors and omissions) coverage? Should you have it? This is becoming a very expensive category of insurance, so many businesses are dropping their policies. You can tell by looking at the policies the type of coverage you are going to need. Chances are you will find insurance is another one of the items that has to be increased, not decreased, as you recast the P & L.

Interest Interest should be a low expenditure. Remember, you are looking at companies that have very little debt, which means spending very little on interest. Of course your interest expense will be higher than the seller's, but at this point I do not want you to add in the additional cost of interest from the financing. Look at current interest on existing financing. The additional interest for new debt service will be taken off the bottom line after you have calculated the value of the seller's company rather than added on here.

Postage & Freight   Such items as postage and freight are rarely the source of any changes in recasting. If you continue to run the business, you are going to pay postage, freight and other such normal operating expenses.

Rent   If you are looking at a company with a rented facility instead of an owned facility, you must look carefully at the terms and conditions of the lease. If it is near the end of a lease term, you will want to see if the lease has "restore to original condition" or "personal guarantee" clauses. If the entrepreneur owns the building personally and has been renting it to the company, he has been using the rent payment as a way of taking out income to avoid withholding taxes. If he has been paying the mortgage principal and interest on the building, you will find a very high rent figure. Whenever you see a deviation from what would be considered a fair market rent for the facility, you want to know why. For example, if it is a 10,000-square-foot factory in the market that rents factory space for twenty-five cents a square foot, and you see the rent on the income statement at a nickel a square foot or a dollar a square foot, it may be because the owner was using it as a way to avoid taxes or because it is a very old lease that is about to expire.

Repairs, Supplies, Taxes, Telephone & Utilities   These are all items you should note, but they are probably not going to be the source of much change when you are recasting.

Travel & Entertainment   Here is where some of the most wonderful entrepreneurial fiction is written. Travel and entertainment will almost always be an item in which by recasting you will be able to find extra dollars for debt service. But you want to be careful that you do not cut travel and entertainment too close to the bone. In many industries the very growth that you are anticipating will require increased travel and entertainment expenses. You may not be taking four vacations a year or going on every industry junket to Bermuda or Hawaii, as Sam did, but you will not want to completely strip away travel and entertainment. It is a valid expense, particularly for you as the new owner acclimating yourself to a new industry or business situation.

Miscellaneous and Bad Debts When I discussed accounts receivable, I mentioned provision for bad debts owed to the seller's business for unpaid bills. This is where you find them. The rule of thumb is, you want to keep the allowance for bad debts at no more than 3 percent of one year's gross sales. If you find a situation in which the actual expense for bad debts has been consistently at 7 percent to 10 percent, or even higher, you know you are dealing with a fairly weak business. This is the kind of business that has been "buying" customers by extending credit to high risks. If you see a situation where there is a rapid increase in bad debts over the past three years, you are dealing with another kind of deterioration. The entrepreneur tried to grow the business and did it by extending credit to even higher risk or fringe customers and it came back to haunt him. Miscellaneous expenses should be consistent and low. If they are not either consistent or low you should ask hard questions: what are they, where did they come from, what is the cause of the variation and how likely are they to be repeated in the future? Again, you are looking for patterns. And you are looking for those expense items in which the owner has hidden his perks. You should be finding typically about $25,000 to $50,000 in owner perks. You want to know how much they cost the company and where he has hidden them in the books.

Net Profit The most important figure in your rescheduled or recast income statement is going to be the pretax net. And that figure, including the deduction for debt service (which is the total payment on all debt, both principal and interest) must be at least 10 percent of the top line or gross revenues or you cannot do the deal. In other words, if you do not give yourself a "cushion" of 10 percent (I would further recommend a minimum of $100,000 on top of the normal operating expenses and the debt service load), the chances are you will not be able to make a go of it in that business. You may at this point have 300 hours invested in the deal, you may love it, but I am telling you, walk away from it. Do not run the unnecessary risk of a failure.

Other Issues in Due Diligence

I have already stressed the importance of using a good attorney and a good accountant in due diligence. Specifically, you want your attorney to look at the Uniform Commercial Code filings for the candidate company to find out if there are any undisclosed, secured debts and to check out the litigation record to see if the seller has a record of being involved in numerous lawsuits in the last few years.

From your accountant you may want to get a businessman's audit of the business. This is not a full audit. It is not going to cost $30,000 or $40,000, but it is going to require that you spend some money in order to have your accountant check some key areas that may be beyond your technical expertise when you are doing your first LBO.

Do not overlook the useful role of appraisers. If there are substantial or unusual fixed assets, get independent, third-party appraisers to confirm the asset values and to support the financing package that you take to the asset-based lender.

You must do your own homework on those three legs of the milking stool: the sales and marketing, the operations, and the finance and organization. The deal has to pass your gut test. These are the key issue areas involved in any business and you have to be satisfied that the business is going to make it if you buy it.

What are the main marketing issues? Every company is in business because it is either better, faster or cheaper than its competition. Very rarely will the owner actually know why his customers are buying his product or service. He may think he knows but until you have talked to some of the existing customers, you will not really have a clear idea of whether they are buying it because it is better, faster or cheaper.

Pay attention to whether you are dealing with a concentrated or fragmented industry. I have already indicated that you should avoid the industry if it is not fragmented. The problem with the concentrated industry is that you do not have control over your pricing.

You are going to want to ask yourself four questions. Do I have here a unique product or service: is it really different? Is there a market for this good or service? Is there a strategy, an effective way of reaching that market? And, can I hold on to current market share long enough to get out of this deal, that is, pay off the financing and hang on to the company for five years? It is this last question, or rather the failure to address this last question, that creates so many failures in leveraged buyouts. You need to buy a company with a dominant position in a niche market because you will have to protect pricing and hang on long enough to your market share to get your money out of the deal. You do not want to go into a situation where the pricing is opportunistic or where the business depends on one or two dominant customers. If you find one customer accounting for more than 10 percent of the sales of the company, it is not a good candidate. I looked at a company once up in San Francisco in which fully 67 percent of its sales went to the telephone company. This kind of a situation makes the company far too vulnerable should that preferred customer ever change its mind and find another supplier or decide that you are simply making too much profit and decide to pay you less. Opportunistic pricing is related to sales based on special contacts, family ties, friendship, lack of real competition or the superstar-type sales personality. If the key people leave or the key relationships change, then the company is very vulnerable. What about the susceptibility of foreign competition? You cannot be in a high- or low-tech manufacturing or distribution business these days without being aware of and concerned about foreign competition.

What are the key operations issues? You do not want to buy a company that has a sole source supplier. Everything that you get in the way of supplies or services should be able to be obtained from other suppliers. You do not want to leave yourself vulnerable to a sole source. You want to know whether the suppliers are going to transfer the credit arrangements when you take over the company. You are looking for essentially mundane product lines with some proprietary aspect; you are not looking for high levels of technology that require frequent influxes of new capital or high levels of research and development.

You are looking for low levels of technology and low labor force skill levels. You do not want to buy a business that requires that you hire sixty engineers as opposed to sixty sheet metal workers. You want to look for a company where there is a pattern of low personnel turnover and training costs, or where you will be able to minimize turnover and training costs. Generally, you want to avoid union situations. You also want to avoid situations where the regulatory environment is negative or is going to turn negative. This is particularly true in any industry that is handling hazardous wastes or requires federal, state or local permits and frequent inspections to continue to operate.

What are the key organizational issues? One of the principal issues is who is going to stay and who is going to leave. The seller will have a very poor idea of who is actually going to stay and who is actually going to go. It will be up to you to make some determination along the way. Another key issue is that you are going to have to find out if there is among the existing employees a general manager candidate. For this to happen easily you are probably looking for a company that has a minimum of twenty full-time employees. The reason I say this is that, typically, managers are effective managing no more than about six people. It is possible for factory foremen to increase their span of control to as many as twelve or thirteen workers, but generally at the management level you are looking at one manager for every six employees. Therefore, in a twenty-employee organization you should have approximately three managers. Out of those three managers you should be able to find one who is ready to step into the role of general manager. You are looking for the person who has the capacity to manage managers. There are critical growth points in the development of a business that occur at roughly the $2 million level, the $8 million level and the $20 million level. If you find a company in one of those three levels of annual revenue, you will want to look very thoroughly at existing management personnel to make sure that you have the horses to pull you through to the next level.

How about contacting these people before the acquisition actually occurs? Generally, I would advise against it. It is a bad idea. In the first place, you have tipped the hand on the issue of employee confidentiality by letting them know there may be a sale pending. In my experience, you are not going to have very accurate information. If you find good, loyal employees, they are going to err on the side of protecting their boss and the company. If you find unhappy employees, they are going to err on the side of distorting the negative aspects of the business. It is not a bad idea to try to locate one or more senior level former employees. I suggest that you attempt to do this. Former employees frequently will not have had the opportunity for an exit interview. If you provide them with the opportunity to have a good "let it all hang out" session, indicating your interest in the company, you may frequently find information that you would not otherwise be able to surface even by asking hard questions of the seller.

I have provided a comprehensive list of due diligence questions—the hard questions to which you must have hard answers—in the Appendix. As you read through this list, it will become clear that you do not have to ask each and every question about each and every candidate business you examine. However, the more you ask at this point, the more you will know. And that knowledge may save you from making a very costly mistake.

4

How Much Is It Worth?

Value, like beauty, is in the eyes of the beholder. By this point you should have a very good understanding of your LBO candidate business. You should understand its risks and the opportunities it offers. Now it is time to answer the question: how much are you going to pay for it? And to answer that question, you must first know how much it is really worth, and what the seller wants for his business.

Fair market value is defined as that price at which a willing buyer will buy and a willing seller will sell, neither being under any compulsion and both having a reasonable knowledge of all the facts. This is what you could call the best of all possible worlds. In the real world you will rarely find such an ideal situation. When I mention the seller's expectations of what his business is worth, you must understand that the seller will not have, in most cases, an appraisal or an evaluation from an independent third party. It is not in the nature of the typical LBO candidate to have gone to such trouble. He will have expectations that are nothing more than ideas based on industry norms, or rumors about competitors' sales, conversations overheard at trade association conventions, or bits and pieces he knows about publicly held companies in the same industry. You will also find that the LBO candidate has a love of round numbers: $1 million, $3 million. He loves the way those big, round numbers roll off his tongue when he is bragging to his friends. You rarely ever see a deal done at $1,000,497. When I bought Sam's business, the price was $1.4 million.

The seller will not have given much thought to the process of coming up with a price. It will be your responsiblity to educate him. In this process you must keep his expectations in mind. They will influence, but not determine, your calculations of value. If you find that the seller is inflexible on the issue of price during the negotiations, it is a tip-off that either you have not done your educational job well or he does not really want to sell. In other words, you have not qualified him properly as a real seller. When you are dealing with a real seller, price is really a nonissue. I know that seems a little strange, but as we go through this chapter you will understand why the price of a business is really not an issue for a motivated seller.

How do you look at this situation? When you buy a business, you are making an investment. The value of an investment is determined by the rate of return for the level of risk in the investment. When you invest in a business, your only return on investment is the profit of that business. I mean the pretax net profit. It does not matter that you have very little or none of your own money in the deal. If you buy a business for $1 million, it is your $1 million investment, whether you borrowed the money or took it out of your piggy bank. It does not make any difference, because after the leverage is repaid, it will be your asset free and clear. You will have bought it for $1 million. You need to be concerned about the price you pay because that will determine whether or not it is a good investment.

There are many approaches to valuing a business.

• *Liquidation Value.* I mentioned liquidation value in our discussion of the balance sheet. That is the net value of the company's assets when sold at auction less its liabilities. If you are serious about buying a company as an LBO, I suggest that you go to a liquidation auction. You can find them advertised in the Sunday newspaper. Depending on where you live, the time of year and the state of the economy, you may find as many as two or three pages of auction notices. Those that are liquidations of companies will clearly say so. Go and become familiar with the process and the liquidation values of fixtures, equipment, vehicles, machinery and other items that are sold at auction. These liquidation values are significant because they are the values that will be used by asset-based lenders as a basis for their lending to you in your leveraged buyout. But these are not the values that should determine the purchase price.

• *Replacement Cost.* Replacement cost is a concept of value that is used by the insurance industry. It is useful as a rule-of-thumb guideline to check out what it would cost you to start the LBO candidate company from scratch instead of buying it. For example, if you were going to buy a machine shop and it had three lathes, one of which was twelve years old, one seven and one three, you would want to know what the replacement cost of those lathes was and not what it would cost to buy them new. Net replacement value is the expected cost to replace the assets of the business minus the total liabilities. This is a very difficult concept to use on retail and services businesses, but it is useful for you to remember.

• *Comparable Sales Value.* The practice of valuing businesses based on an analysis of comparable sales of other businesses entered business appraisal from the business opportunity brokers who were recycled real estate brokers trained to look at comparable sales in the evaluation of income properties. However, in valuing an LBO candidate, you have an apples-and-oranges problem when trying to use the comparable sales approach. In the first place, you may be trying to compare the sales of public versus private companies, or very small companies versus larger companies. Then there is the issue of whether you are dealing with a complete interest or a partial interest, or whether it is a forced, estate sale or a normal, free-will sale. It is very, very difficult to get accurate data on privately held business sales in the $500,000 to $10 million range. So even if you could find comparables on which to base your analysis and if you could resolve all of the other issues, you still would find it hard to get enough comparables to come up with an accurate value for your LBO candidate. You should be familiar with the concept only inasmuch as it may have shaped the seller's expectations. If he was down at the country club and heard that Fred had a brother-in-law in Wichita who sold a "similar" business for $10 million, you may be in trouble if he feels that his "similar" business should be worth the same. And you need to be in a position to educate him as to the problems and difficulties of the comparable sales approach to value.

• *Net Present Value.* The best approach has consistently proved to be net present value. What I mean is the net present worth in current dollars of the expected future cash flow produced by the business over a specified period of time. You are going to leverage the company for five to seven years, which will typically be the length of a long-term debt on the balance sheet. Net present value is based on the idea that a dollar is worth more today than it will be a year from today. It is the old "bird in the hand is worth two in the bush" principle. The dollar in your hand today is less risky than the dollar that might be in your hand a year from today. And there is the inflation factor. Even if you knew for certain that that dollar a year from today would be in your hand, you would still have to deduct from its value some amount to reflect inflation. The dollar that is due to you in a year is going to be worth less. How much less will be a function of the amounts deducted for risk and inflation. How much you decide to deduct will be based on such real world factors as prevailing interest rates and such measures of inflation as the Consumer Price Index. It will also depend on how you feel about the riskiness of the business. Just how you calculate the value of the risk will be covered a little further on in the chapter.

First, let me show you a specific method of valuation

for determining a purchase price based on the net present value approach. The place to begin is with the rescheduled balance sheet starting with net worth or book value, or what is also called shareholder's equity. For all of these calculations, it will be necessary to use the recast balance sheet and P & L. Remember that net worth is determined by subtracting the liabilities from the assets to arrive at the net worth or book value of a company. To put this method of valuation in perspective, the average price of all companies traded on the New York Stock Exchange is one and a quarter times their book value. Typically, privately held companies in the $500,000 to $10 million range will sell for one to two times their recast book value.

When you recast a balance sheet and adjust all of the asset values to their present fair market worth, take the bad debts out of accounts receivable, get rid of obsolete inventory, clean up the notes receivable and put the fixed assets down at their replacement values, you can determine the real, tangible net worth of the company at current market value. While this is not the whole answer to the value of the company, it is the place where you must start. You have to know the net current assets and the net long-term assets of the company in order to determine its tangible net worth at current market. This is where you begin to set a realistic purchase price for the company. If you arrive at a price that is at or below net working capital (current assets less current liabilities equals net working capital) it is a very good deal. If you are trying to set a price and the seller has his own ideas about the value of the assets, remember that the higher depreciation on the higher asset value will affect the price. You are going to buy the assets on a dollar-for-dollar basis. Where you are going to pay a multiple is on the earnings. To really understand this, you must also be familiar with the earnings- and cash-flow-based techniques for determining the value of a business.

The main reason the balance sheet approach alone will not give you an accurate picture of total value is because it does not reflect any value in the earning power of the assets. Remember that there are only two real values for an asset: one of them is its financeable value as collateral in the eyes of an asset-based lender and the other is its earning power measured in terms of the profit it will give you. This is why you have to consider earnings and cash flow techniques. The most common of these is the price/earnings ratio. It is the one used to describe publicly held companies, and that is why it is the least relevant to determining the value of privately held companies. Publicly held companies and privately held companies are managed for different goals. The managers of public companies want to maximize earnings, while the private entrepreneur wants to minimize taxes.

Income capitalization is the key to value in an investment (I mean here income as stated in terms of pretax net profit). To capitalize the income you must pick a rate of return, because buying the business will be your investment. For example, assume you have decided you want a 10 percent return. A 10 percent rate of return means that you would get 10 percent of your money back each year or all of it in 10 years. This is your rate of capitalization (cap rate). In this example, you take your cap rate of 10 and multiply it times the pretax net profit, say $100,000, and you come up with a price of $1 million. That is the income capitalization technique. This is a concept that comes from real estate and is used in the evaluation of income-producing properties. However, in order to use the income capitalization approach in the valuation of businesses you must compensate for the difference between an all-cash sale and a debt-financed sale because the cost of money (interest on the debt) will change the return on investment. So, if you are going to use income capitalization as a quick check on price, remember to compensate for this difference between a cash sale and a debt-financed sale.

Discounted cash flow is another method of evaluation that is frequently used because it produces some reliable, accurate results. The discounted cash flow theory begins by saying that the company is worth the present value of its anticipated future cash flow for some period of time, typically five years. In order to calculate this, it is necessary to project the cash flow for a specific period. Since I have been using the five- to seven-year period for long-term debt in financing the company, I will use a five- to seven-year period for the cash flow projections. Once the cash flow has been calculated, it is then necessary to calculate the net present value for each year's cash flow by selecting the appropriate discount factor based on the rate of return you are seeking. You can pick this up from the tables in a standard textbook in your local library. The primary problem with this approach is that it is very time-consuming and does not really give you the most accurate picture of value because you are dealing here with cash flow and not pretax profit. It is a step in the right direction, but it is not going to give you the best approach to price.

• *Excess Earnings Method.* The best approach to determining the value of your LBO candidate is called the excess earnings method. Excess earnings is basically a very simple concept. If you make an investment you expect a return. For example, if you have your money in a savings account paying a 10 percent rate of return and you find a bank that is paying 12 percent on the same kind of account, the difference between the 12 percent and the 10 percent, that 2 percent difference, is excess earnings. You would be carrying 2 percent more than you had expected for the same kind of investment. Excess earnings are earnings above and beyond what would be expected from an investment of a similar risk level.

The excess earnings approach to valuing business starts with the rescheduled income statement after all the expense adjustments have been made. When the adjustments have been made and you have completely recast the income statement, you will now have an adjusted pretax net income figure. It is this figure that is the source of the calculation of excess earnings. Remember, the only return on your investment in a business is the profit of that business. Only by calculating the excess earnings can you see if you would be getting a real return on your investment.

Beginning with the adjusted pretax net profit figure from the bottom of the recast income statement, go back now to the recast balance sheet. On the recast balance sheet you take the current assets and subtract the current liabilities to get the net current assets. Since there is a risk in buying a business, which is greater than the risk involved with a "safe" investment such as U.S. Treasury bonds, you are going to insist on a rate of return on your investment in net current assets that is higher than the yield on the bonds. Remember, you are buying the assets of the business, the net current assets and the net long-term assets that make up the net tangible worth. If you are buying them, you are making an investment in them. And if you are making an investment in them, you have a right to a return on that investment. If a "safe" risk-free investment is returning 10 percent, then your rate of return should be higher to compensate you for the higher risk. Current assets are those that can be turned into cash within the next twelve months. They are reasonably liquid, which is why they are called current assets. The level of risk in buying current assets is higher than buying a government bond but not so high as buying the long-term assets, which is why you deal with them separately.

For this example, assume that you need a 12 percent return on the net current assets. Take current assets minus current liabilities to come up with a figure for net current assets. Now calculate 12 percent of that figure. Next you turn to fixed assets and subtract long-term liabilities, which is going to give you net long-term assets. Since these assets are not as liquid (they cannot be turned as readily into cash), you expect a higher rate of return on your investment in them. What rate of return? I suggest 15 percent. So you are using 12 percent to determine rate of return on the net current assets and 15 percent to determine the net long-term asset rate of return.

HOW TO CALCULATE EXCESS EARNINGS

RECAST PRETAX NET PROFIT		**$270,000**
(from recast Income Statement)		
Total Current Assets	$740,000	
(from recast Balance Sheet)		
less Total Current Liabilities	$510,000	
(from recast Balance Sheet)		
NET CURRENT ASSETS	$230,000	
12% RETURN ON NET CURRENT ASSETS		**$ 27,600**
Total Fixed Assets	$303,000	
(from recast Balance Sheet)		
less Total Long-Term Liabilities	$ 38,000	
(from recast Balance Sheet)		
NET LONG-TERM ASSETS	$265,000	
15% RETURN ON NET LONG-TERM ASSETS		**$ 39,750**
EXCESS EARNINGS		**$202,650**
NET CURRENT ASSETS	$230,000	
NET LONG-TERM ASSETS	$265,000	
ADJUSTED NET WORTH	$495,000	
(Also called BOOK VALUE)		

Now you have two figures, one for each type of return on your investment in assets. Subtract both of these figures from the adjusted pretax net income, and that remaining profit equals excess earnings. If there are no excess earnings once you have subtracted your return on investment from the adjusted profits, you are not making an investment. You are buying a job. The business itself will not provide a return on your investment.

To be a true investment, the business you buy should provide you with two types of return. First, you should get a return for the investment in the assets—the machinery, equipment, fixtures, vehicles, inventory, accounts receivable and, if it's included, cash. Second, you should get a return from the operations of the business above and beyond your return on the assets themselves. This second kind of return is generally called the "goodwill" value of the business. However, "goodwill" has a precise accounting definition that your CPA can explain. For our purposes here, it is better to think of this second type of return as coming from excess earnings.

Once you have completed recasting the seller's balance sheet, it is a relatively simple matter to arrive at the net current value of the assets. You may be able to do it without the help of your accountant or outside independent appraisers. If the assets are worth $300,000, then you will be paying the seller $300,000 for the assets. In other words, you will be paying the seller dollar for dollar on the value of his assets.

Calculating the value of the excess earnings is more complicated. Excess earnings are really a stream of profits above and beyond the return you expect from the investment in assets alone. The source of this stream is sales to customers. This may seem simpleminded, but it is the reality behind such vague terms as "goodwill" or "the good name of the business." What is really meant by these terms is that there are customers, people or firms that are accustomed to buying goods or services from the seller's business. Your problem in determining a fair price for the business is to set a value on that stream of profits. So the solution must address the issue of how reliable or risky is the continuation of that stream.

If you decided that the present customers were not

very likely to continue to buy from the business and no new customers could be found after the first year, then the value of the excess earnings would be one. In other words, if the stream is going to dry up at the end of one year, then the value of the stream can be no more than 1 times a year's excess earnings. This would be an excessively risky situation since it would require you to recover 100 percent of your investment in excess earnings in a year. Even if you stretched it to two years (2 times excess earnings) it would represent a 50 percent annual return, which is what you might expect in high-risk venture capital or other speculations.

This process of multiplying the expected return in excess earnings by the number of years in which you expect to recapture your investment is called capitalization. You are capitalizing an income stream or turning a flow of profits into a fixed value of capital. When you multiply the earnings by the number of years, the multiplier is called a cap rate. In most of the businesses you will be evaluating, you are going to capitalize the excess earnings at a rate of return somewhere between 20 percent and 25 percent. A return of 25 percent would be a cap rate of 4. In other words, you are expecting to get your money back in four years (4 times 25 percent equals 100 percent). A 20 percent return would give you a cap rate of 5 (5 times 20 percent is 100 percent).

In effect, this process allows you to say that the excess earnings stream is stable enough to allow you to get your investment back in four or five years. If you find a situation where the rate of return should be as high as 33 percent (a cap rate of 3), you may not want to do the deal. The seller may want you to go as high as a 6 or 8 cap rate. This may be because he is confusing this process with the price/earnings multiplier common to the stock market. The P/E ratio is not the same thing and is really useful only for publicly held companies. Your calculations are going to determine the capitalized value of the seller's excess earnings. If this still seems a little confusing, I want you to follow me through this example very carefully.

A Step-by-Step Example of the Excess Earnings Method of Determining the Value of a Leveraged Buyout Candidate

Start with the bottom line from the rescheduled income statement: the recast pretax net profit. It is now going to be moved up to the top line. In the example, the figure is $270,000.

From the recast balance sheet you take the total current assets for Sam's company ($740,000) and subtract the total current liabilities ($510,000) in order to arrive at a figure for the net current assets ($230,000). I should point out, parenthetically, that another term for net current assets—total current assets less total current liabilities—is working capital. For the purpose of determining excess earnings and the purchase price, we are going to refer to it as net current assets. And in this case we have net current assets—that is, assets that are cash or can be converted into cash in less than a year—of $230,000.

Because of the liquidity of current assets, you are going to expect a lower rate of return on your investment in net current assets than you would expect on the net long-term assets. I suggest that you use a figure for the rate of return on net current assets of 120 percent of the one-year T-bill rate. The 120 percent figure will compensate you for the higher risk of an investment in net current assets of a business compared to an investment in U.S. Treasury bills. For the example, let's assume U.S. T-bills are yielding 10 percent. So you should look for a 12 percent return on net current assets. Calculate 12 percent of $230,000 and get a figure of $27,600. That is the return you should be getting for investing in those assets. Now subtract that $27,600 from the recast pretax net profit.

Next you are going down to total fixed assets of $303,000 and from that you subtract the long-term liabilities. If you are dealing with a good LBO candidate you should be subtracting very little long-term debt. In this example, you only subtract $38,000 in total long-term liabilities to come up with net long-term assets of $265,000. Because net long-term assets, by definition, are less liquid than current assets (and, therefore, more risky), you are going to have to get a higher rate of return on your investment in them to justify the higher risk. I suggest that you use a figure equal to 150 percent of the one-year T-bill rate. For our example, that is 15 percent. On the net long-term assets, 15 percent of $265,000 is $39,750. You subtract that from the $270,000 recast pretax net just as you did the earlier figure. When you subtract both your 12 percent return on your net current assets and your 15 percent return on your net long-term assets, you end up with a bottom line figure of excess earnings, $202,650. In other words, Samco produced $202,650 beyond a rate of return that justifies the risk of owning the assets.

The very fact that there are excess earnings lets you know that this business is showing an actual return on investment in the business itself above and beyond the return on investment in the assets of the business. The excess earnings in Sam's company is $202,650. In order to take excess earnings and convert it into a range of purchase prices, go back to net current assets, the $230,000 figure, and add that to the net long-term assets, the $265,000 figure, and you come up with $495,000. That is the recast book value or net worth of the company. You are going to pay Sam dollar for dollar on those assets, or $495,000.

Now, how do you use the excess earnings figure? First, you multiply it by a capitalization rate of 4. Take the $202,650, multiply it by 4, and get $810,600. Then multiply it by 5 to come up with $1,013,250. Now add those figures (the excess earnings multiplied by 4 and the excess earnings multiplied by 5) to the adjusted net worth of $495,000 and you come up with a range of $1,300,000 to $1,500,000 and loose change. Remember, I mentioned that entrepreneurs

HOW TO DETERMINE A PRICE RANGE

	25% Return (Cap Rate of 4)	20% Return (Cap Rate of 5)
Excess Earnings	$ 202,650	$ 202,650
times Cap Rate	4	5
	$ 810,600	$1,013,250
add Adjusted Net Worth (Recast Book Value)	495,000	495,000
Round off to Price Range	$1,300,000	$1,500,000

like to deal in round numbers, so I am rounding those off. This is the range of purchase price you can afford to pay for that business as an investment. And you see what I mean when I say that you will pay dollar for dollar for the assets and a multiple for the earnings.

Business evaluation is an art and a science. There is no such thing as a formula that gives you an exact answer for the value of the company. Furthermore, the result that you get by applying the excess earnings method must come up with a range that matches the seller's expectations of what his business is worth.

I have reviewed several approaches and balance sheet, cash flow and capitalized earnings methods. However, I recommend that you stay with the excess earnings approach. In Internal Revenue Service ruling 5960, at least nine different guidelines are given for the determination of value of privately held businesses, but the IRS recognizes the excess earnings approach as being the most useful and the most valid. It is the one that is going to get you into the least trouble as you approach your first LBO.

To summarize briefly, recast the balance sheet, then reschedule the income statement to arrive at a pretax net profit. Using the pretax net profit as a point of departure, determine what your rate of return should be on net current assets and what a higher rate of return should be on your net long-term assets. Next, subtract the two of those from rescheduled pretax net to arrive at excess earnings, and capitalize your excess earnings. I suggest that you stay with the 4 or 5 cap rates. You should avoid situations that require such a heavy rate of return that you feel you should use a cap rate of 3. When you come up with a range of possible prices, match it to the seller's expectations. If it looks as if you are within the same ballpark, then you are ready to proceed to the next stage of the process.

Remember that value, like beauty, is in the eyes of the beholder. And that the seller's expectations are going to be conditioned by industry norms, rules of thumb, conversations he has heard in the coffee shop or after hours. He will not have investigated the situation thoroughly. He is not going to have had a professional appraisal done on his business. You are going to have to educate him. In order to educate him, you need a good, solid understanding of the risks and opportunities of the business and how to approach the correct pricing of the business. But, as a buyer, regardless of the seller's expectations, return on investment can be your only criterion. You must accurately value the assets and calculate the return. You must determine the excess earnings accurately. You must determine what the correct capitalization rate is. You should have a thorough understanding of the strengths of the business and a real gut-level feeling that lets you determine the level of risk and the rate of return you are looking for as you make this investment.

If all this still seems a little mysterious to you, I suggest that you go back over it two or three times until it begins to clear up. Once you have understood the concept of excess earnings, it really is the most simple, direct way to come up with the value of a going business, and lets you set an accurate approximation of purchase price.

Let's assume your price range and the seller's expectations are close enough to proceed to how you can put together a deal that satisfies the seller's needs.

5

■How to Structure the Deal

If you do not satisfy the seller's needs, you will not be able to close the deal. In order to structure a deal that works and put together an offer that is acceptable to the seller, you must meet his needs in a reasonable, satisfactory manner. I do not mean indulging his every whim and wildest fantasy, but it is important for you to identify very early on what the seller really needs and wants out of the sale of his business. You must do this before you can begin work on structuring a deal offer that will be acceptable to him.

Whether the seller mentions it or not, the most important underlying issue will be security. After all, he has been with this business fifteen, twenty, even twenty-five years. He will be undergoing a major change in his life-style. Even if he is tired, bored, burned out and ready for something new, he is still going to be losing the security of the business that has been providing him with a good living for many years. In a typical transaction there will be a 25 percent cash down payment and the remaining 75 percent will be financed over five to seven years. The seller will have an understandable concern about the security of the rest of his money. Can you actually pay it to him? Is it really going to be safe? These are a seller's concerns. He is going to worry about whether or not you can run his business well enough to make those payments.

Beyond security, the seller's needs are going to fall into four main categories:

- Regular income
- Concerns about estate planning
- The need for cash now
- The longer-term need for tax-sheltered income

It is up to you to identify which of these categories is the most important to the seller. Then you must structure a deal that meets his needs in each of these areas of concern. If the deal you structure requires outside financing, remember that it must also meet the lender's needs. You may be involved here with only a seller. The leverage has got to come from somewhere, and if it does not come from the seller, there will be a lender. I will take you through the lender's needs and how to meet them in a later chapter. I do want to bring to your attention that you may be satisfying more than just the needs of the seller, but at this point I am going to focus on how to structure a deal to meet the needs of the seller.

An important word of caution concerning deal structuring: Do not create a "fraudulent conveyance." This is your responsibility, not the seller's. If you do create a fraudulent conveyance, both you and the seller will end up regretting it. Since you are putting the deal together it is up to you to structure it legally. Fraudulent conveyance is a legal concept that comes out of federal bankruptcy law. It is based on the concern that creditors have in the exchange of the ownership of a business. Suppliers, those companies that provide the goods and services that keep the business operating, do not normally demand quarterly or monthly financial statements and credit reviews of their customers. Some of them may monitor the change of ownership. They may even change the terms and conditions on which they have been extending credit to the company you are buying.

But by and large, those suppliers will continue extending credit to you without a review of creditworthiness. It is because those suppliers rely on the continuing creditworthiness of the business that the concern about fraudulent conveyance arose in the first place. The result was some federal bankruptcy legislation.

Basically, what the law regarding fraudulent conveyance says is that if you buy a business and you and the seller agree on terms for a sale that involve so much debt that one or both of you could have known and should have known that the company would not be able to survive and make its debt service payments, then you have created a fraudulent conveyance. For example, you are buying a company that has been doing $3 million in sales for the past ten years and showing a $150,000-a-year pretax net. In order to make this deal work you convince the seller, yourself and everyone else that the sales are going to go up to $7 million, and that is how you justify all the additional debt in order to pay the seller. You have set up one of the basic preconditions for a fraudulent conveyance, because you have no basis in the company's history to project more than a 100 percent increase in sales. You would be very unwise to project increases in sales above and beyond normal industry growth and something for inflation. But projecting sales too aggressively is not the only way that you can create a fraudulent conveyance.

Anything you do in structuring the terms that burdens the company with debt above and beyond its capacity to pay, given its normal operating realities, runs the risk. If the company goes bankrupt within the next two years, a judge or a trustee in bankruptcy can declare the sale a fraudulent conveyance. If that happens, then the seller is going to have to put all of the proceeds of the sale back into the company. And you, as the buyer, are going to have to restore all of the assets to the company and return all of the money you have borrowed against them or got when you sold them off. The lender will lose its senior security position on those assets that it lent money against, so that the unsecured creditors (the suppliers who show up as accounts payable on the balance sheet), have a fair, equitable shot at the assets of the company in the event it is liquidated in the bankruptcy.

Your potential liability for a fraudulent conveyance covers the first two-year period. Most sellers will not be aware of this. This does not remove them from the obligation and responsibility. That is why it is your concern that you do not create a fraudulent conveyance. It is also another reason why you want a good, deal-oriented attorney and a good, deal-oriented CPA involved. Because one of the questions you are going to ask them is, Have I put together a deal here that could be construed as a fraudulent conveyance should the company go into bankruptcy in the next two years?

The concept of "win-win" is not just a nice phrase or kind consideration. "Win-win" is really "win-win-win-win." The buyer, the seller, the creditors and the lender must all win in order for there to be a successful LBO. If any one of these parties ends up in a position where it can lose, the deal can fall apart or, more likely, not be done at all. So you have to meet your needs, you have to meet the seller's needs, you have to meet the needs of the lender and you have to be aware of the rights of the unsecured creditors, the trade suppliers who are providing the credit that shows up on that balance sheet as accounts payable.

Your Financial Tool Kit

I want you to think about the techniques of deal structuring as financial tools. Imagine that you have a tool kit filled with these financial tools that will help you to structure deals that work. Now, take a look into your financial tool kit and see what you have to put these deals together. There are two kinds of tools: those that create cash and those that defer cash payments. Each deal you look at will require five or six of these tools in order for you to put together a deal that will be acceptable to the seller because it meets his needs. I want you to become familiar with all the tools in the kit. And I want you to continue to look for others as you progress beyond your first LBO. It is to your advantage to keep that tool kit filled and up to date. It is OK to experiment. Do not be afraid to try new techniques that you hear about, read about or pick up from other LBO buyers you meet. Do not get stuck using the same two or three tools in every deal you try to do, because you are going to limit your effectiveness if you do.

Cash-Creation Tools Cash-creation tools are going to come from the balance sheet items, particularly assets. We are going to start with the assets by their nearness to cash. That means that we start with cash. In most cases, the seller is going to sell you his cash for tax reasons. Remember, if he takes the cash out of the company it will be treated as dividends. He will pay corporate tax on the earnings and he will pay personal income tax on the dividends when they are distributed.

Accounts Receivable

You factor accounts receivable. You go to a factor. You find them in the Yellow Pages. You can either sell the accounts receivable or borrow against them. I am only referring to viable accounts receivable, accounts that have been due for less than ninety days where the goods or services have actually been delivered. The issue with the factor is recourse. If he buys your accounts receivable without recourse, you are going to get less money for them than if he has recourse to you. In other words, if one of the accounts you factored to him turns out to be bad, he can bring it back to you for either a credit or replacement. That is called recourse. You are going to get slightly more money from the factor if you borrow against your accounts receivable than if you sell them outright. If you borrow against them you are going to create a debt and you will have to service that debt. The payments will have to come from somewhere. If you sell your accounts receivable, the disadvantage is that the customers will receive notification from the factor that the factor is now in possession of the account and payment should be made directly from the customer to the factor. In some industries this would be unacceptable because it is not a common practice. It would cause too much concern among the customers if their accounts were sold to a factor. In other industries—for example, the garment industry—it is simply the way business is done. Everybody's accounts are factored. In many industries, the factor acts as the credit department. If the factor is unwilling to take the credit risk, then the company knows that it is dealing with a customer that is not creditworthy. The amount of cash you can raise by factoring accounts receivable will vary from 50 percent to 80 percent, depending on the industry, the size of the company, the accounts themselves, even the time of year and prevailing interest rates.

Notes Receivable

There are two things that you can do with notes receivable when they show up on a balance sheet. You can either sell them or you can look through the actual provisions of the note to see if there are grounds for calling the note. Many times, notes receivable will have a provision that allows for accelerated payment on the part of the note holder if certain terms and conditions are not met. You should read through the note to see whether the terms and conditions have been met and whether there is a reason here for calling that note receivable. When the note receivable is sold, it could be sold at a discount or at a premium, depending on the terms of the note and particularly its yield. If it had a very low interest rate and the prevailing interest rates at the time you go to market are high, then you are going to have to discount it. But if this is a note that was made at a time when market rate interests were 18 percent, and the current market is only 12 percent, then you may be able to get a premium beyond the face value for the remaining balance of the note. Look for ads in the classified section of the Sunday newspaper. In some cities, such as Los Angeles or New York, there are several columns of ads from individuals and institutions who buy, sell and trade notes receivable, second Deeds of Trust, second mortgages and such paper. They will be the people who will tell you what the current market condition is, what that note receivable might be worth and whether you have to discount it or can get a premium for it.

Inventory

There are several approaches you can take to inventory, because inventory means several different things. For example, in a manufacturing company, inventory means raw materials, it means work in progress and it means finished goods. All three of those are inventory. For a retail store, inventory means the goods on the shelves plus the ones in the back room. For a wholesale distributor, inventory is the cases of goods on the shelves, where an open case usually indicates broken or damaged goods. In a service business, you usually have very little inventory at all. Because inventory means so many different things, you are going to have to take into account the type of business you are trying to buy. Generally, there are five approaches you can take with inventory. There is a propensity for sellers to use the inventory account as a way of hiding assets in order to lower their tax burden. You will frequently find inventory the most controversial asset on the balance sheet. To avoid controversy, if the seller indicates that the inventory is worth way more than the book value, one of the things that you can do is to let the seller keep the inventory. Let him retain ownership of it. If he tells you his business is worth $1 million and the $100,000 book value of the inventory is wrong, that the inventory is really worth $500,000, let him keep it. Do not argue with him. Simply subtract his

$500,000 value of the inventory from the $1 million purchase price and lower the purchase price. You have just created half a million dollars in cash. This is what I mean by cash-creation technique. So let the seller keep it. Here are the terms on which you are going to let him keep it. You agree to keep it for him rent-free. You agree that you will only buy inventory from him. You agree not to go to another supplier, but you will not be obligated to buy all of his inventory from him if some of that inventory is not selling. This arrangement will keep you from having to buy dead inventory, unwanted goods, those items the seller fell in love with but simply could not move. It is like a consignment.

The second thing you can do with inventory is to sell it back to the supplier, as I did with Samco. Good, saleable inventory in its original condition is always worth something. I do not mean going into a retail store, gathering stuff off the shelves, throwing it into a bag and sending it back to the supplier. It would have to be in its original packing carton in a saleable condition. Clearly, you have to deal with a willing supplier in order for this to happen. But it does happen.

The third approach to inventory is to put it onto a consignment basis from the supplier, which is different than allowing the seller to keep it. The supplier gets paid only as the inventory is sold. That gives you the inventory to operate the business, particularly in a retail situation, but does not obligate you to pay for it until it has been sold. There is no account payable for consignment inventory.

The fourth thing you can do with inventory is call in an inventory liquidator and liquidate the inventory. The Yellow Pages of most phone directories will contain scores, if not hundreds, of inventory liquidators, auction houses, professionals who will come in, give you a realistic, quick value for the liquidated price of that inventory and handle the actual liquidation.

And finally, you can borrow against inventory. This is

applicable primarily in manufacturing businesses because most retailers and wholesale distributors have already borrowed against their inventory in the sense that there are accounts payable against that inventory. If there is unencumbered inventory, you can borrow against it. Take the actual value of the inventory and subtract the accounts payable against that inventory; then the unencumbered net value of the inventory can serve as collateral for a loan. Particularly in manufacturing businesses, you can borrow up to 25 percent of the value of finished goods and 40 percent of the value of raw materials. Work in progress has virtually no collateral value.

Fixed Assets

If accounts are the number-one asset that asset-based lenders like to see, machinery and equipment is the number two item on their hit parade. There are three ways you can create cash from machinery and equipment:

- Let the seller keep it and lease it back from him, as you did with the inventory.
- Involve the company in a sale-leaseback to an independent third party that structures such arrangements.
- Borrow against it. Generally, machinery and equipment can be borrowed against at the rate of 80 percent of its liquidation value. You will have to get an independent third-party appraisal to satisfy the asset-based lender when you determine what the liquidation value is.

There are a couple of things that you can do with real estate if there is property in the deal. If you do find real estate in the deal, one of the first things that you should know is that you are dealing with a seller who has been poorly advised. Most sellers will have found that it is better for them to own the real estate as individuals and to rent or lease it to the company, because they need the depreciation in order to shelter some of their own income. If you find a situation where the real estate is owned by the company, you are dealing with a less than fully sophisticated seller or some problem exists. You need to ask questions to determine why the real estate is still in the company. In a quick sale or a liquidation, you would get 50 percent of the market value of the real estate. You can borrow against the real estate from asset-based lenders at 65 percent to 70 percent of its market value. There is another technique that would allow you to get considerably more cash out of the deal. It is a little complicated, so I want you to follow me carefully as we go through the steps, but this approach does work. It will get more cash than either the quick sale or the asset-based loan.

The first step is to have the seller buy the building from his corporation at fair market value (not its book value, but its current fair market value). He buys the building from the corporation as an individual. The seller gives the corporation a note (an IOU) for the entire purchase price. With one hand, as an individual, the seller gets the title to the building and with the other hand he is giving the corporation a note. You, as the buyer of the corporation, sign a new lease with the seller as the owner of the building. It has to be a twelve- to fifteen-year lease of the kind that is called triple net, CPI, which requires the tenant to pay all taxes, repairs and utilities. The CPI portion of it refers to the Consumer Price Index, which means that the rent is indexed for inflation. This permits the rent to increase automatically with increases in the cost of living. So it is a triple net, CPI lease. It must be for twelve to fifteen years. The corporation, with you as the new owner, signs the lease to rent the building from the seller as an individual. The seller then sells the lease at a discount to a pension fund or insurance company. They buy the lease from him. On a twelve- to fifteen-year lease there will be enough cash in the deal so that even on a discounted basis the lease will produce at least 100 percent of the purchase price. Now the seller no longer has the lease but he has the cash. The pension fund or the insurance company that bought the lease has the lease and it will be the landlord. Your new corporation will be paying its monthly rent to the pension fund or the insurance company. The seller now redeems the note, the IOU he left in the corporation when he bought the building at the first step. The seller goes to the corporation, gives the corporation the cash and gets back the IOU.

This must be an arm's-length transaction. The seller could not have done it without you, because the IRS would come in and say this is simply a sham transaction done in order to get the real estate out of the deal. The IRS will disallow it. The seller needs you in there as the buyer of the corporation to sign that lease. This technique turns the real estate into cash and gives the seller a nice built-in tax shelter because he owns the building. Since it was sold at a market rate, he now has a very high basis for depreciation. This way you are able to help him shelter some of the income that he is going to get from the sale of the business.

Deferral Tools   When you look into your financial tool kit for cash-deferral tools, the most useful are perks, the same indirect compensation the seller has been taking out of the business. I have already mentioned perks, but I want to review them again because they are the most overlooked item in the financial tool kit when it comes to deal structuring. Frequently they are the most important, because when you get to the step in negotiating the deal where you ask the seller, "What are you going to miss most about this business after you have gone?" in most cases the first thing that seller is going to mention is one of his perks: his car, his annual trips to the industry convention in Bermuda, his company airplane, his membership at the country club or whatever toys he allowed himself. This is fine from your point of view as the buyer because providing perks does not show up on your balance sheet. Furthermore, continuation of perks can help in a neat and orderly transition. By building in three, four or five years' worth of perks, you can dangle a carrot in front of the seller in order to keep his interest in helping you own the business. Perks are also useful in helping to ease the seller out of the business. After all, if all he has to give up is coming to work and he still gets to keep the money and the perks, it may be easier for him to let go. By continuing those perks for five years you will have given him a transitional period in which he can financially and psychologically adjust to his new life. Typically, the perks for the seller in the $500,000 to $10 million business category are going to run $30,000 to $50,000 a year. Those are pretax dollars, and the seller is going to know that it would cost him $60,000 to $100,000 in after-tax dollars to provide those same perks for himself after he has sold the business. If you continue a $30,000 to $50,000 perk package for five to seven years, then you have just knocked $150,000 to $350,000 off the purchase price. Another way to look at it is that you have just created an off–balance sheet liability, a non-interest-bearing loan of $150,000 to $350,000. Remember, when you are thinking about the continuation of perks, the seller must be an employee of the company. It is virtually impossible to continue perks for a nonemployee. This consideration will figure into some of our later discussions when we are considering other cash-deferral tools.

Debt

What about existing debt? Debt is already a deferred item. When you deal with debt you have four tools that you can use.

• Refinance short-term debt into long-term debt. Lenders will usually go along with you because they are going to get a higher rate and probably points for making the loan. By refinancing the short-term debt into long-term debt you reduce the cash flow required to support the payments on that short-term debt. If you take $10,000 that is due this year and stretch it into $10,000 that is due over five years, you have greatly reduced the cash required year by year to repay that debt even though the interest rate has gone up. The other thing you will have done is to increase your working capital, because you have reduced short-term liabilities. Working capital is current assets minus current liabilities. So if you have lowered your current liabilities you have increased your working capital.

• Assume debt. Although most banks will not go along with this, under certain circumstances, other lenders will allow business debt to be continued with a change of ownership. Many loans have a provision that if there is a change of ownership or other material change in the business, the debt is immediately due and payable. The bankers call the loan. You are going to have to find out what the terms of the debt are, and you will have to satisfy the lender that they should continue the debt in order for you to assume it. You would handle this in the same way you approach an asset-based lender, which I will cover in the next chapter.

If you find a situation where the debt is to the seller as an individual—the corporation on its books shows that it owes money to the seller as an individual because the seller has "lent" money to the corporation—you are really looking at equity. The seller set the "loan" up this way to be able to draw money out of the corporation as something other than dividends. The easiest thing to do here is simply tell the seller, "Cancel the debt because I am buying your real net equity in the business."

• Collateral substitution. You can find alternative collateral to free up the assets that are securing existing debt. Examples would be the equity in your home, the equity in other real property that you own, stocks and bonds, anything else of value that could be substituted as collateral for that which was being provided by the business. When I bought Sam's business, the zero coupon bond was a form of collateral substitution. The effect is that the assets of the business are no longer collateralizing the debt. The zero coupon bond is substituted as the security for the debt.

Installment Notes

Another tool that you will use frequently is an installment note. The issue with installment notes is security. I advise you to use an annuity as a means of providing security for installment loans wherever you can. Not all insurance companies will guarantee the yield on their annuities to maturity. Some will only guarantee them for five years, so it is necessary for you to check around at the time you are actually looking for one. Call several companies. It is a good policy to keep in touch with the lenders and the financial market in order to keep your tools up to date. You should know what the prices and terms of these tools are so that you always have the most recent information as you approach the deals.

The other issue with installment notes, at least in the mind of the seller and the lenders, will be whether you are talking about senior debt or subordinated debt. It is a matter of who comes first and who comes second. It is the same as a first mortgage or a second mortgage on your house. Who has the first right to the asset? A junior or subordinated position still has some security because the loan advance rates of the asset-based lenders are so strict. In a case where the asset-based lender is providing you with a loan of 75 percent of the liquidation value of the machinery and the equipment, there is still 25 percent in there. If you are talking about half a million dollars' worth of machinery and equipment at liquidation value, then there is $125,000 of equity left that the seller should be willing to accept. This is an element of negotiation, whether that seller is willing to take a subordinated or second position in any installment note that he takes back. With installment notes, keep in mind the possibility of collateral substitution. Is there anything outside of the assets of the company that you can offer for substitute collateral?

The same issues apply to balloon notes. The only difference between balloon notes and installment notes is that with a balloon note the entire sum is due at the maturity of the note. Security will be the issue, and I advise you to use the zero coupon bonds. As I indicated previously, there are three types of zero coupon bonds: those issued directly by the U.S. government, those that are issued by agencies of the U.S. government such as Freddie Mae or Fanny Mae, and those that are issued by major corporations with AAA credit ratings.

You can use these bonds in a structured sequence. You could take a $100,000 five-year bond, a $100,000 ten-year bond, a $100,000 fifteen-year bond and a $100,000 twenty-year bond to have a sequence of balloon notes if deferring the entire balloon amount for twenty years was unacceptable, or if the seller's cash needs were staggered in that manner through time. One of the things to watch for with the zero coupon bonds is that the older issues will have higher yields but are callable. If you are looking for the true twenty-year security, you do not want to be in a bond that the government can call (pay off at its option) at any time before the twenty-year period. In order to get a twenty-year bond that is actually going to be good for the entire twenty years and not be redeemed, you are going to have to settle for a little lower yield. It may cost you 1 percent or 2 percent more to get a long-term bond that is not callable. In a zero coupon bond the interest actually accrues annually. Remember they work the same way as the Series E savings bond. You buy them at a discount from their face value and the interest accrues until the bond matures. The interest accrues annually but is not paid to the bondholder. You put the zero coupon bond in the seller's name because it is the security for his balloon note. It is his bond and the Internal Revenue Service considers that it is his responsibility to pay the taxes on the interest that accrues each year. Under current regulations, taxes on that interest are due and payable each year. It is not your responsibility to inform him of his tax liabilities.

Royalties and Earn-outs

A couple of other cash-deferral techniques I want to take up now because they are similar are royalties and earn-outs. These are cash-deferral techniques that you will find very useful in the right situation. Royalties are used when there is a question of value on a new product that has been developed by the seller's company but has not yet actually been tested in the market. In such a situation, research and development will have been finished, the prototype tested and ready to go, but no one knows how the product is really going to do in the market. Software and technology companies are frequently in this position. The technique here is to let the owner retain ownership of that product and pay him royalties as a percentage of gross sales upon collection. You are buying the rights to sell that product on a royalty basis from the owner. You are going to give him a percentage of the gross sales when you actually collect the money. You never set up a royalty agreement on the basis of net profit and you never set up a royalty agreement on the basis of when the product is first sold, only when the money is actually collected. You never want to do it on net profit because you do not want the seller looking over your shoulder and telling you how to run the business. It is simpler to calculate the royalty if you give him a percentage of gross. You can find out in a few phone calls what a royalty agreement should be for your industry. It could be anywhere from .5 percent to 15 percent. There is no way of coming up with a rule of thumb that covers all industries. You will have to do some research to find out what royalty arrangements are applicable to the industry in which you are operating.

Earn-outs, on the other hand, are useful in a situation where there is no specific product or service but the company is poised to take off. The seller has convinced you there is a great opportunity in his company. You know that the company has only had sales of $2 million a year for the past five years, but you have done your research. You agree with the seller that this company is about to leap up into the $10 million range. But you are prudent. You are cautious. You are careful. You do not want to pay for that projected growth until you have actually realized it. There is a question in your mind. It may happen. You believe that it will happen. That is why you are willing to buy the business. But you are not absolutely positive for sure, so you structure an earn-out in which you agree to give the seller a percentage of the increase in gross sales over the average growth for the past three to five years. If the company really has had sales that averaged $2 million a year for the past five years and you really do get an increase up to $10 million, then you would be giving the seller the right to participate in that growth by giving him a percentage of the $8 million above and beyond the first $2 million. You do not specify the $8 million figure obviously, but you do specify a percentage. You will have to do some research and negotiate with the seller in order to arrive at a percentage that is fair to the seller and to the company. Obviously, you cannot give away too much of your gross and still operate the company. But you can find out what the industry standards and norms are.

Agreements with the Seller

I am going to conclude my discussion of cash-deferral techniques with a look at not-to-compete, employment and consulting agreements. They are used similarly and frequently interchangeably in structuring deals. A not-to-compete agreement has to be a part of every deal that you structure. Typically, the seller agrees not to compete with you and the company you are buying for a period of three years, and the agreement covers only similar goods and services in similar markets. You cannot afford to have that seller running around out there in a position to go into competition with you. But the Internal Revenue Service and the courts have held that not-to-compete agreements have to be reasonable. A not-to-compete agreement is an expense item for you, as the buyer, but for the seller it can be taxed either as ordinary income or as capital gain, depending on the deal structure. It is necessary for you to assign a dollar value to the not-to-compete agreement so that the IRS will not come in and impute a dollar value to the agreement. If they do, they are going to take a look at the three highest years' income that the seller made over the last five years and average that three years' worth of income. They impute to the three years of the not-to-compete agreement the average income of those three highest years, because you are paying the seller not to work. The IRS reasons that he should get paid for not working at a job as much as he got paid in his best years for working at the same job. In order to minimize the tax impact on the seller, you are going to assign a very small dollar value to the not-to-compete agreement, especially if you are worried about goodwill. The difference between the book value of the company and what you have agreed to pay for it (the purchase price) is goodwill. You cannot depreciate goodwill. If you can take a high dollar value and assign it to the not-to-compete agreement, you can eliminate some of the goodwill. But you must be careful, because the seller may have to pay ordinary income on that. If he does not know or it is not a problem for him, then you can go ahead and load up the dollar amount on the not-to-compete agreement in order to eliminate most or all of the goodwill that you ordinarily would have to carry on your books.

You want the seller to sign an employment agreement, but a smart seller will avoid one. If the seller has any good counsel at all, he will not accept an employment agreement, because an employment agreement is a personal services contract. It is embedded in the body of the documentation for the deal and can be a deal breaker for the seller. From your point of view, it is easy to provide the perks for the seller as an employee but very difficult if he is not an employee. So if you feel that a good perk package is a substantial part of the deal you are structuring and you believe that the seller will not check with a good attorney, then you want to include an employment agreement to make it easy to provide those perks. Employment agreements do not appear on the balance sheet. You have here yet another off–balance sheet liability at no interest rate. It is usually a footnoted item if you are going to the extent of providing financial statements with footnotes.

Consulting agreements, on the other hand, normally allow the seller to set up a separate company. If he is well advised, he will have done this. Because it is an agreement with a separate entity, it allows the seller to provide you with his own services or with substitute services of a like quality. It is not a personal services contract. This becomes important to the seller and should be important to you because in the one out of five deals that fall apart due to misrepresentation or some other issue, it is a failure to perform on the employment agreement that the buyer uses to get out of the deal. In most cases, the seller just stops performing the consulting services and the buyer has a basis to go into court and set aside the entire transaction because the seller was not performing under the employment agreement. With a consulting agreement, the seller has the opportunity to continue providing the services through another person.

Here is a wrinkle that you may want to consider on consulting agreements as a deal-structuring tool. It is based on the principle that you do not pay taxes on borrowed money. Specifically, the seller does not have to pay taxes on this money because he is borrowing it from the company. Now, the way he gets the money to borrow is that you prepay for several years' service. You know that he is going to get income and it is going to be ordinary income under the not-to-compete for three years. So you are not going to be able to provide much income under the consulting agreement during those three years without putting him into an unfavorable position. But suppose that you had a ten-year consulting agreement that was set up so that at the end of the third year payments escalated from a very small amount, say $5,000 or $10,000 a year, to $50,000 or $100,000 a year in the fourth through the tenth year. And suppose that you, as the buyer, prepaid the entire 10-year contract. Then the seller borrowed that money from his own company to use or invest. The seller would not have to pay taxes on that money until he had actually earned it, but he would have the use of the money up front from the beginning. This is a very, very attractive way to provide a lot of cash on a tax-sheltered basis to a seller who has a need for immediate cash from the deal but does not want to pay taxes on that cash even at a 20 percent capital gains rate.

The final aspect of consulting agreements for you to know about is that it is very difficult to provide a continuation of perks to the seller if he has set up an independent company to provide a neat and orderly transition as a consultant rather than as an employee. Remember as you review this material on deal structuring that a deal that works begins with satisfying the seller's needs, especially his concern for security. Remember not to create a fraudulent conveyance and remember that perks are the number-one tool and are the most frequently overlooked.

How I Bought Sam's Business

Now I am going to take you step by step through a sample deal. This is the Samco deal that I have already mentioned to you.

A Note of Explanation:
As we go through this example you are going to read such statements as "I sold this asset, I discounted that asset and borrowed against that." You should be

aware that I am referring to activities that happen within the escrow agreement prior to the closing of the deal. When you bought your house, you opened an escrow account with a buy-sell agreement and instructions that went into escrow. The agreement said you were going to make a down payment of 20 percent and the balance would be a new mortgage loan and that the closing of the deal would be subject to your ability to obtain the financing. Businesses in this $500,000 to $10 million range are bought and sold in the same way. We call it a trust security account instead of an escrow account, but there is a buy-sell agreement. When you open the trust security account with a buy-sell agreement you also put in a conditional letter of commitment from the lender who will be providing the money secured by the assets of the company. This conditional letter of commitment says that if the assets are as they have been represented and if they are appraised at the values indicated, then the lender will provide the money that he said he would provide. In other words, the deal is subject to the financing. You are not really selling the assets or borrowing against them during the trust security account period. What you are doing is arranging the financing, so when I say that I have decided to sell this or borrow against that, I am referring to actions that are made in these conditional letters of commitment. You would not really take assets out of the company because you do not yet actually own the company. The $10 million deal is about the largest-size deal that can be done with a buy-sell agreement in a trust security account. Above $10 million, these deals get too complex. The financing is so complicated and takes so much time to put in place that they really cannot be done within the normal time frame of a trust security account. That is why you read about the Ted Turners, the Carl Icahns and the T. Boone Pickenses using junk bonds. It is easier and quicker for them to go get the financing they need with the junk bonds, buy the company, and then finance the assets and pay off the junk bonds. The deals are done exactly the same way in terms of the principles of leverage, but the timing is different. Here we are talking about deals that are much simpler to do than Ted Turner's proposed leveraged buyout of CBS, because the financing is so much simpler.

Now let us take a look at the Samco deal.

I am going to start with the assets at the top of the balance sheet. Generally, you would look to the assets in the balance sheet for the down payment. Then you would look to the income statement to provide the debt service payments. This is because the typical terms of a sale are 25 percent cash down payment and the balance financed at interest over a three- to seven-year period. You will find deals in which you can generate the entire purchase price from the assets on the balance sheet. You will also find deals that require no down payment. The entire purchase price can be financed from the future cash flow of the business. In this type of a deal you would only need to look to the income statement to structure the deal.

Start at the top of the assets. Remember, assets on a balance sheet are organized by their nearness to cash. So you start with $40,000 in cash. Why would a seller sell you his cash rather than just put it in his pocket? It is a tax consideration. Under the current tax laws, if Sam took $40,000 in cash out of his business, first he would have to pay corporate taxes to the federal and state governments, then he would pay personal income tax on that same money as distributed dividends. Sam would have been lucky if he put twenty-five cents on the dollar into his pocket as a result of that transaction. By selling his cash to you as an asset of the business, under current capital gains tax treat-

SAMCO DEAL STRUCTURE

Assets on Balance Sheet		Cash Value	(%)	Cumulative Cash
Cash	$ 40,000	$ 40,000	(100)	$ 40,000
Accounts Receivable	$428,000	$ 342,000	(80)	$382,000
Notes Receivable	$ 38,000	$ 32,000	(85)	$414,000
Inventory	$235,000	$ 117,000	(50)	$531,000
Fixed Assets	$286,000	$ 215,000	(75)	$746,000

	Value to Seller	Cost to Buyer
Down Payment	$ 350,000	$350,000
20-Year Installment Note	$ 350,000	$122,500
20-Year Balloon Note	$ 700,000	$ 70,000
Five-Year Perk Package	$ 150,000	
	$1,550,000	$542,500

"War Chest" Cash	$ 746,000	
less Cost to Buyer	$ 542,000	
	$ 203,500	Cash in Business

* Deferred cost of $30,000 a year for five years as interest-free loan that is not reported on buyer's balance sheet.

ment he is going to put eighty cents on the dollar into his pocket. That is why Sam sold me his cash. So you start out here with $40,000 in cash.

Go on to accounts receivable. Remember, these are just around the corner from cash. In Sam's business there were $428,000 in accounts receivable. There was also a note receivable, in this case a loan to an employee. It was secured by a second mortgage on the employee's home for $38,000. It was not really a useful, productive asset of the business. Of course, the employee was making regular payments, so it was producing interest. But in terms of the operation of the business it was not a useful, productive asset.

There was an inventory of $235,000, and that brought

the value of total current assets to $741,000 on the balance sheet. Then you go to long-term or fixed assets and see that there was furniture and fixtures at $22,000. This was the current book value. The equipment and machinery were carried at a book value of $223,000, and the vehicles were being carried at $41,000, which brought the total fixed assets to $286,000. Other assets in this particular example were prepaid deposits, but they did not figure in as a source of financing for the deal. Other assets are reported separately because there is no likelihood that they are going to be converted into cash. So the $17,000 in other assets was unavailable. But it brought the overall total assets to $1,044,000.

Here is what I did with those assets in order to generate cash to come up with a down payment. I started with $40,000 in cash. The accounts receivable were sold to a factor at eighty cents on the dollar. A factor is a financial entity. It could be an individual or it could be an institution. In this particular case it was an institution that bought the accounts receivable. The other thing I could have done was to borrow against them. When you sell accounts receivable to a factor, you get roughly eighty cents on the dollar. So I raised $342,000 from selling those accounts receivable to the factor and added that to the $40,000 cash that I began with, which increased the "war chest" to buy Sam's business to $382,000. Next was the note receivable. Because it was not a useful asset to the business I decided to sell it. Because the interest rate was low compared to the prevailing market rates at that time, I had to sell the note at a discount and was only able to get $32,000. That $32,000 cash was added to the war chest, bringing the total here to $414,000.

Then there was the inventory. There are at least four different approaches to creating cash from inventory. I will cover all of them in detail later. In this particular case, half the inventory was sold back to the supplier at a discount. Now, this was not the entire inventory. This was inventory that was not needed to run the business. After my analysis of the business I determined that there was too much inventory; it simply was not moving that fast. The supplier was willing to take it back because there was a discount of 10 percent offered. The supplier knew that ultimately the business would be repurchasing that inventory at full price in order to operate. He knew he would make his money back. Since the supplier wanted to keep me, the buyer, as a good customer, he went along with the deal. After all, the business had been a good account for many years. In this case, the supplier was willing to buy back $120,000 worth of inventory for $117,000. This brought the war chest up to $531,000.

So far I had not borrowed any money at all. I had sold the accounts receivable to a factor. I had sold the note receivable at a discount to a private individual as an investment. I had sold half the inventory back to the supplier for cash. But I was still short on my war chest to cover the $1,550,000 purchase price I had negotiated on Sam's business. So I had to turn to the fixed assets because it was the first item of actual debt I had to take on to do the deal. I financed all of the fixed assets—furniture and fixtures, equipment and machinery—with an asset-based lender who provided a loan of 80 percent of the actual value, that is, the liquidation value of those assets. Such lenders look to the "hard" value of those assets as a basis for the credit. They provided a five-year loan for $215,000 at prime plus three. That $215,000 was added to the war chest and brought the total up to $746,000. That was the total cash I created in the business within the terms of the trust security account in order to buy the business.

It is important for you to keep in mind when you are doing leveraged buyout deals that the seller sets the price, the buyer sets the terms, and the terms drive the deal. After lengthy negotiations, Sam had agreed to accept a purchase price of $1,400,000. Sam agreed to accept a 25 percent down payment, so $350,000 of the $1,400,000 would be coming to him at the closing in the form of cash. He also agreed to an installment note making regular monthly payments over a twenty-year period for a total of another $350,000. The remaining balance of $700,000 he agreed to get at the end of twenty years in the form of a one-time balloon payment note. That was $350,000 down, $350,000 payable in equal monthly installments over twenty years, and $700,000 as a balloon note payable at the end of twenty years. He was understandably concerned about the security of that 75 percent of his money that was going to be financed over twenty years. So it was up to me to satisfy Sam's needs for financial security. In this case, the reason for the structure using the installment notes and the balloon note was Sam's estate planning considerations. He did not have a great need for a lot of cash now. He had estate planning concerns for his children. That is why the deal was structured in this way.

To provide Sam with his $350,000 cash down payment, I took $350,000 in cash from the $746,000 war chest created in the escrow account because the cash down payment must be made in cash. The twenty-year installment note was secured by a single-payment premium prepaid annuity. This is an insurance product that guaranteed payments every month for twenty years until the entire $350,000 is paid. I bought it at closing for a single premium, prepaid on a one-time basis for thirty-five cents on the dollar of the total due over the twenty years. It cost me $122,500 at closing to provide Sam with $350,000 in equal monthly payments over twenty years. The insurance company was the third party who guaranteed the payment. Sam did not need to look to me or to the business for the security of that note. That was very important to him, because if the business burned down or I got hit by a car and was unable to pay, what was Sam going to do? He had sold his business and might not get paid for it, so his security concern was very high. By using the annuity with the payment guaranteed by a major insurance company, I was able to satisfy much of Sam's concern.

His other concern was about that $700,000 balloon payment note. In order to secure that, I bought a twenty-year U.S. Treasury bond. This was a zero coupon bond. It works the same way as the Series E savings bonds. As I remember them, you bought them for $37.50 and they matured in seven years for $50.00. The zero coupon bonds work the same way. They are available directly from the government or from government agencies or from major, triple-A corporations such as IBM or AT&T. A twenty-year zero coupon bond was purchased for ten cents on the dollar—in other words, it cost me $70,000 at closing to buy a bond that would mature for $700,000 in twenty years. Because the liability for the payment was shifted to a third party, in this case the United States government, Sam had no concern about the viability of that payment. For a cash cost to me of $542,500, Sam was given a purchase price value of $1,400,000, and the company was left with $203,500 in working capital in its account to operate the business.

At the last minute, Sam got a bad case of seller's remorse when it actually came to giving up his baby. So I increased my offer to $1,550,000 by agreeing to keep Sam on as an "employee" for five years and paying his life insurance, health insurance, automobile expenses and country club dues and fees. This perk package cost me $30,000 a year for five years, which added $150,000 to the $1,400,000. This made the deal for Sam. And I could pay it out of future cash flow. It was just like an interest-free loan from Sam to me for $150,000 that did not show on my balance sheet.

■How to Finance the Deal

$$\text{\$}$$

The golden rule of leveraged buyout financing is easy to remember! He who has the gold makes the rules. As the buyer of an LBO with little or none of your own money in the deal, it follows that somebody will be providing the money—the leverage in the LBO—in order to make the transaction happen. In most cases, the seller himself will be the lender. He will provide the money in the form of seller carryback financing as installment or balloon notes. However, in some deals it may be necessary for you to finance the deal with an independent third party. What you will be looking for is an asset-based lender.

To a lender an LBO is nothing more than another investment opportunity. Your LBO must compete with all other potential investment options in terms of expected return, risk level, liquidity, exit potential and other factors. In the best of all possible worlds, the LBO lender is looking for a strong, clean balance sheet with lots of good assets, assets that are easy to identify, easy to appraise and easy to liquidate.

The lenders are looking for little or no preacquisition debt. They know that their debt will be on the balance sheet after the acquisition. It is the preacquisition debt that they will be looking at, particularly debt other than accounts payable to trade creditors and suppliers. There should be virtually no debt other than the accounts payable. If there is, as a first-time buyer of an LBO, I would suggest that you think about passing on the deal. It may be just too much of a debt burden unless you have structured the deal in such a way that it requires very little additional debt.

As far as the company is concerned, the LBO lenders will be looking for a company with steady, profitable sales. They will look for a company that has good market position. Simple products, loyal employees, low turnover and low skill levels are also attractive. Nonunion situations are particularly appealing.

When they look at you they want to see a seasoned pro with lots of successes, lots of experience and a strong financial statement. But that is in the best of all possible worlds. You are going to be dealing with reality, yours and that of the company you have picked.

When you approach lenders, you approach them on very much the same terms that you first approached the seller. Your first impression is going to set the tone for the entire transaction. So, as a successful businessperson, you act the part. You are going to act in a strong, confident way. You are not hesitant. Nobody knows it all, and lenders are particularly concerned about the person who has a hair-trigger response to every question. Be open to their input. They are going to notice whether or not you hear their suggestions, criticisms, or anything else they may have to say. Remember, they are going to be your financial partners for a rather long period of time. If they provide the long-term leverage for your LBO, they are very likely to be with you three to seven years. From the beginning, you should be building a relationship.

When you go be fully prepared. Nothing says "amateur" more surely than a lack of preparation. Be sure to pick the right lender. Have a good, strong plan when you go.

What Kind of Lender Do You Want?

I want you to imagine a continuum of credit for LBO financing. On one end of the continuum is the 100 percent secured loan with the assets of the business as collateral. The lenders at this end of the continuum would look entirely to the assets for the repayment of the loan if there was a default. At the other end of the continuum you have 100 percent cash flow. The lenders at this end of the continuum do not care what the assets are. They look entirely at the cash flow generated by the business in order to determine whether they think the loan can be repaid.

Along the credit continuum, you will find all of the players in the leveraged buyout financing field. Not all of them have the same rules, nor do they all operate in the same way. For example, you have the secured versus the unsecured types of financing. The secured LBO financers normally want a senior lien on the assets. They want the equivalent of a first mortgage. Unsecured lenders take that position because they want everyone, themselves and everyone else, including the trade creditors, to be at risk. Normally you find unsecured lenders in the larger, more complex deals.

There are some advantages to the unsecured-lender approach. In the first place, it is normally easier to cash out the seller when you have the funds advanced by an unsecured lender, because more funds can be advanced than the secured lender is usually willing to provide. The unsecured lender usually takes an equity position, so that there is not as much leverage being provided. This eliminates a little of the risk involved in the deal. Finally, suppliers providing credit through accounts payable normally are more comfortable with a transition that is financed by an unsecured lender because they are not at as great a risk. The assets are not secured, so they are available in the event that something should go wrong in the operation of the business.

What Kind of Deal Do You Have?

Now, let us take a look at several types of loans and see which kinds of players might be involved as the LBO lenders in each of these types of deals. The first one is the situation where there is adequate collateral for the entire loan. There is a poor cash flow. There is no clear turnaround plan, and the buyer's plan here is to redeploy the assets of the company. This kind of deal would be taken to small commercial finance companies that you would find in the Yellow Pages of your phone directory. Your bank, your deal-oriented attorney or CPA can direct you to them as well.

The second deal is the kind in which there is adequate collateral. Again you have poor cash flow, but you have a management team that has a well-documented turnaround plan. This company looks as if it could actually experience some growth over the next five years. This kind of a deal would be attractive to the larger commercial finance companies, such as Westinghouse Credit, GE Credit, ABCO, Heller International or Talcott Associates. These are companies you could find in the Yellow Pages. You might also consider the secured lending units of sophisticated banks. They usually advertise in the *Wall Street Journal* and the financial pages of the local business press.

The third type of deal is one in which you would find adequate collateral and a good, strong, clean balance sheet. But you also have a good cash flow. Any secured lender is going to take a look at a deal like this.

With poor collateral and weak cash flow but a good, solid, well-documented management plan for a turnaround, there are a limited number of sophisticated lenders and investors in the LBO fund and venture capital community that could be interested in such a deal. However, as a first-time buyer of an LBO, you might lack the credibility with these sophisticated lenders and investors to convince them that you could execute the plan unless your track record included one or more successful turnarounds.

With poor collateral but a strong cash flow in the deal, the larger money center banks and major regional banks could be approached if you have a proven track record as a manager or entrepreneur.

Finally, if you have put together a deal that has poor collateral, weak cash flow, no turnaround plan and a game plan that is simply to redeploy the assets in a kind of internal liquidation scenario, good luck! I do not think you are going to find any lender who is going to go along with you.

As a first-time buyer of an LBO, you are seeking financing primarily from commercial finance companies as opposed to banks. Now, banks have lower rates than the finance companies due primarily to their lower costs of money. Banks get their money from depositors and at a fairly low average cost compared with the rates at which finance companies finance their operations. Typically, the finance companies will get two to seven points above and beyond the bank's prime rate. So if the bank's prime rate at the time you are looking is 10 percent, you can expect the finance companies to be quoting 12 percent to 17 percent. Both banks and finance companies look to get their money back in three to seven years. That is their exit plan. They expect the loan to be entirely repaid. That is how they are going to get out of the deal.

Banks are going to look to you for creditworthiness and guarantees. They may even want additional collateral. It is not unusual for them to suggest a second mortgage on your house or the pledging of stocks, bonds or retirement funds. Certainly they are looking for personal guarantees, perhaps cosigners. Finance companies that are asset-based lenders do not view their fully secured asset-based loans as risky propositions. They approach the situation differently than do banks. They are not looking to you as an individual for creditworthiness; they are looking to the assets of the business.

How Do You Find a Lender?

If the deal is within the $100,000 to $5 million range, you are looking at a small- to medium-size commercial finance company that functions as an asset-based lender. At this point you, as the buyer, have two options. You can either package the financing for the deal on your own, or you can work through a broker or loan packager. If you decide to go through a broker or a packager, make sure that you get several recommendations from sources that you trust. Be sure to check out references. There are many people out there posing as loan brokers and packagers who will take fancy front-end fees. They want to be paid up front and will do nothing more than put together a package of papers that will not go anywhere. If you are going to work with a broker or a packager, be sure to work with someone who has a track record of actual success in your kind of deal. You want someone who has done asset-based LBO deals in the size and price range of your deal.

What do you pay them? You give them, typically, 3 percent of all debt money they raise and 5 percent of any equity money they raise. You provide for their fees out of the proceeds of the financing upon the successful completion of the deal. You do not pay them anything up front— not a processing fee, not a fee for preparing the plan. They work strictly on a success fee if they are the honorable, ethical and successful loan brokers or packagers that they have represented themselves to be and that you need in order to get your deal financed.

Over the last twenty years, asset-based lending has diverged into two different, distinctive lending philosophies or approaches. Both types have their advantages and disadvantages to you as the potential borrower. Regardless of type, asset-based lenders as a group are not in the business of financing liquidations. So once they are convinced that the business will make it, their lending decisions are going to be based on the nature, quality, value and marketability of the assets of the company.

Let us look at the two types of secured lenders. The first I would characterize as the "old school." The old school of secured-lending philosophy is based on the notion that since the borrower (you, as the buyer of the LBO) cannot obtain unsecured credit, the reason for them, as the secured lender, to make the loan in the first place is that it must be based on downside collateral coverage. Every penny of the money they advance to you must be recoverable from the collateral, the assets of the business.

The primary disadvantage in working with the old-school-type secured lender is that there is really not as much leverage available due to their security concerns. If they are only willing to advance 50 percent to 75 percent of the value of good, hard assets, there will be a lot of potential leverage there that just is not going to get financed. Certainly you can see that a more aggressive approach or more ambitious formula would yield more money for you.

The advantages to you, however, are even greater than the disadvantages. Since the old-school-type asset-based lender is fully collateralized, should you experience a temporary downturn in the operation of the company or in the economy as a whole, this lender is not going to panic. He is going to be able to ride it out with you because he is fully covered. In the worst case, if the company fails, the lender is protected. He is not going to come after you. Generally, old-school-type secured lenders do not require personal guarantees because they have already determined that you are not worthy of unsecured credit. Since they have this full downside protection, this type of secured lender is not entitled to an upside share. They get no equity kickers. They do not participate in higher rates of return. They get what they agreed to get and that is two to seven points over the bank's prime rate.

Let us compare that with the corporate-finance type,

the newer type of secured lender. The corporate-finance school of secured lenders relies primarily on the LBO's projected cash flow to repay the debt. If you are an anxious buyer waiting on the sidelines wanting to get your deal done, this approach can be very attractive. You can save a lot of time not waiting around for appraisals to be finished and the rest of the lender's due diligence to be completed.

After the deal is closed, however, there is a much greater risk to you as the borrower. In the event of a downturn, this type of lender will try to force the loan balance down by calling the loan. He will not ride along with you as will the old-school secured lender. This increases your level of risk considerably. Moreover, this type of lender frequently requires personal guarantees and upside participation, usually through an equity kicker. As a first-time LBO buyer, you'd do best to find an old-school asset-based lender that does not require personal guarantees or equity participation.

Where Do You Find a Lender?

I would begin with the National Commercial Finance Association. That is the trade association of asset-based lenders based in Manhattan. You could call them or write them for their membership directory. I would start there, calling local offices of the asset-based lenders that are members of the association. You should check with a deal-oriented attorney or a deal-oriented CPA and any local bankers or other members of the financial community you know to get some recommendations.

Make sure you get involved with an institution with which you feel comfortable as well as with an individual there who can get the job done. It is not easy to identify these individuals. It is not always a function of their job title. You want to find the person within the organization who can work with you. You are looking for someone who is really a mover and a shaker, someone who can get your deal through their internal process and get it closed. The best course of action is to check within the local financial community to find out which players have the best reputation not only for helping to structure deals that work in your price range and industry but also for working with buyers after the deals are closed.

Once the euphoria has passed and you own your first LBO, the hard work of running that business is really upon you. You want a financial partner, a lender, who is going to work with you. You have a right to expect some things from the lender. It may be true that there are a number of potential buyers seeking leveraged acquisition financing who do not fit the qualifications for a particular lender. The fact that you fail a given lender's credit screen may be a reflection on you or it may equally reflect on the lender.

Lenders are like designer jeans. The fact that they are well known and highly acclaimed does not mean they will fit you. While the lender might well be paying your cost of admission to the LBO, remember, you are paying part of his salary. You are entitled to be serviced by a lender that meets your criteria. It is an unfortunate fact of life in the credit business that lenders often promise what they cannot deliver. Sometimes they give you a positive indication because of ignorance. At other times they deliberately tell half-truths to keep you on the hook on the assumption that the shorter your time frame and the fewer your options, the greater the likelihood that the lender can bait and switch by restructuring the credit you were initially offered.

Unfortunately, the problem is not always an institutional one. There are many cases where an overly aggressive sales rep of the lender winks at company policy in order to get a deal done. This is particularly true in institutions that pay a commission to their business development people based on their productivity. I want to repeat my suggestion that you begin by checking to see that the institution you are dealing with has a reputation for delivering what it says it will. Also check that the individual you are dealing with has a similar reputation. Once you have done that, you should then determine that you are going to be getting what you pay for. Be a good consumer of credit.

In putting together an LBO you are looking to a lender for two things: the ability to get the deal done and the willingness to stick with you after the deal is done. You want the lender to provide counsel and advice where it is appropriate and to have some staying power if things do not go totally according to plan. Therefore, you have to determine what you are buying for the money you are paying in interest. If you are getting a quick yes and an even quicker bailout in the event of adversity, there is no interest rate in the world low enough to compensate you for the additional risk you are going to be assuming by dealing with a second-rate lender. You should also be aware that a lender will often quote rates in terms of a combination of an interest rate on funds employed, a closing fee for providing the credit facility, an unused line fee covering the difference between the amount of borrowing and the amount of the maximum facility and perhaps an auditing fee, a servicing fee, or possibly even other items. Every lender states its charges differently, so it is critically important for you, as the borrower, to analyze all elements of cost in determining what the actual effective bottom line interest rate will be. You will find substantial variations in both the presentations and in the rates. If you find a lender that has the capacity to get the deal done in a reasonable period of time and that has the desire to work with you in understanding the business and the business plan, that has a commitment to track the business plan after the deal is closed and that has the patience to stick with you if you are operating under a sound business premise but suffering temporary setbacks, then you have found the best of all possible worlds. If you can find such a lender at an effective interest rate that your cash flow indicates you can support, without having to pay an equity kicker, you should not try to look elsewhere to save that extra half a point or so in interest charges.

What a Lender Wants from You

When you go to an asset-based lender, you should know what a lender is going to expect from you. In the first place he is going to want to be comfortable with you as a person. He wants to make sure that you are not crazy and that you are not a crook. Do you act like a businessperson? Do you look like a businessperson? Do you talk like a businessperson?

Once the lender is comfortable with you, he is going to be looking for the answers to three questions. Do you know what you're buying? Are you willing to go at risk on the credit? (Let me add that most lenders like to see at least one third of the buyer's net worth at risk. Now, that is "like to see," it is not "must have" or "will require." Remember that your old-school secured lenders are not going to require this. But they do want to know whether you are willing to personally guarantee the loan.) The third question is, if the lender cannot provide enough funding based on the assets themselves, can you as the borrower find the rest of the money? Do you either have it or can you come up with it? Those are the issues in the mind of the lender before he gets on to making a determination of whether he is going to make you the loan.

Do you know what you are buying? In the beginning, the lender is going to focus on what the company will look like immediately after the deal closes and the new financing is in place. That is the aspect of the deal he is most concerned with. The lender is going to be very concerned with sales. Immediately after the deal closes what will sales be like, especially with key accounts? Are there any key sales people, including the seller? If they leave the business or something else changes that key account relationship may change. Will the sales go elsewhere or diminish or will the terms of payment change? Is there anything else that is going to affect the sales? How about the cash flow?

The next concern will be the suppliers' credit. Are they

willing to continue extending credit to the company after a sale? Are the suppliers going to go along, knowing it is a highly leveraged transaction? Are they going to change the terms or stop supplying the company altogether? The lender wants to be sure that the accounts payable (trade credit) financing is going to be there on a continuing basis.

Another area of concern in the mind of the lender will be the production and operations aspects of the business. Will key people stay? What about labor problems? How many dollars is it going to cost the company just to stay in business and be competitive with their product lines? Are there going to be any problems with the seller leaving the business in terms of a neat and orderly transition? Is there management in place that will be able to operate that business in a profitable way?

The answers to many of these questions depends on how the seller was spending his time in the business. If you look at the typical small business you see that entrepreneurs spend about 80 percent of their time in the operations and production area—wherever it is that the product is made or the service is performed. That is where the seller spends his time. About 15 percent of the time, energy and resources are spent in the financial and administration end of the business in such activities as personnel, payroll, collecting accounts receivable, paying bills, looking for ways to save a buck, etc. Only about 5 percent of the seller's time and energy resources are actually spent on marketing and sales. If you were to ask the seller "Where is the area of greatest opportunity to grow the business?" he would tell you about 5 percent in production, about 5 percent in finance and administration and about 90 percent in marketing and sales. The typical seller is currently spending 5 percent of his personal resources in the area where he sees 90 percent of the opportunity.

A lender in an LBO knows it is true. That is why the issue of sales and marketing is number one on his hit parade. In order to go to that lender and meet his expectations, you have to have a good, solid business plan. The plan must be part of a total package designed for the lender. Most entrepreneurs have an aversion to planning. They do not like to plan. But going through the discipline of planning forces you to think in a structured, thorough way. The purpose of planning is primarily to tell you what not to do. As you are developing your five-year plan for this business, you should consider the various scenarios that you could follow. Then you eliminate the unacceptable or inappropriate. You are trying to find those areas in which you could actually hurt the company by taking it there and eliminating those as possible choices for the company. That is where you begin with a plan.

The Financial Plan

The financial package you give to the lender should include historical financial statements of the company you are buying. These should not be your restructured or recast versions. The lender will be concerned with the actual performance of the company as shown in the balance sheets and income or P & L statements. If you have the cash flow or changes in financial position statements or if you have any audited statements, so much the better. Include them, but at a minimum you must have the balance sheet and the P & L for the past three years.

Your pro forma (pro forma is Latin for "before the fact") projections of your financial statements for the next five years must include balance sheets, income statements and cash flow projections. You are going to be doing all three. The first year's figures should be done on a month-by-month basis. For the second and third years, you should be doing your projections on a quarter-by-quarter basis. For the fourth and fifth years, you will simply be doing annual summaries. I am assuming that this is a typical five-year debt so that five years of pro forma financial statements will be adequate. If you are going for seven-year debt, then you will need a sixth and a seventh year done in annual summary form so that your pro formas cover the entire period of the debt.

You should have a brief history and background of the company and its owners. Make it brief, concise and to the point. Be sure to include in the history and background an explanation of why the seller is selling the business. You should also include an analysis of the market and the industry. You will need to cover such issues as trends in the industry and in the specific markets served by the company. You should also address the dynamics of the industry —what is actually going on, how foreign competition is coming into play, what the long-term cycles within the industry are, what the company's market share is—and give an analysis of its principal competitors in terms of the strengths and weaknesses of their product line, their market position and their marketing approach. You must give the lender a good, clear picture of the market situation and the industry.

You need to present your strategy on how you plan to keep or expand the market share of the company. You will want to include a summary of the proposed financing: how much money you are seeking, how it will be secured, what rate and terms you are expecting and how you plan to repay the debt. If you propose to factor 80 percent of the accounts receivable, then you need to say it. If you intend to borrow 75 percent of the appraised liquidation value of the fixed assets, you need to spell that out. The lender must know what you are thinking about the structure of the financing for your deal.

You must include biographies of key managers and a complete schedule of all the assets. If you are including the accounts receivable, you would include an accounts receivable aging analysis as well. Any appraisals that you have on major capital assets, real estate, machinery and equipment you want to include at that time. Those should be independent, third-party appraisals by such firms as American Appraisal, Seymour Pollock & Associates or Richard

Kittson & Company—the reputable, established appraisal outfits. Remember that graphics—bar charts, pie charts, photos, product literature and copies of ads—all help make the presentation more readable, more immediate for the lender.

I want to return to the issue of strategy. The most inportant element of your business plan is going to be the overall strategy, the operating tactics that you choose. Your overall strategy should be expressed in a statement of no more than three strategic goals that you intend to achieve over the five-year period. These goals imply major lines of activity, things that you want to accomplish over the next five years. I do not mean three per year but three goals over the entire five-year period. As an example, suppose you chose as strategic goal number one your desire to increase sales by 10 percent a year. At the end of five years this will give you a 36 percent share of your primary market. That is a strategic goal. It does not tell you how you are going to get there. You may have to reposition your bottom-end product line into a middle-market product line through pricing. Or, your goal might be that you want to reorganize your manufacturers' rep form of marketing and distribution to an in-house factory-based sales staff. This would also be a strategic goal.

Operating tactics are the straightforward, itemized lists of the steps you are going to take to meet your strategic goals. When you are preparing this statement for your business plan, do not get bogged down in details. You should be able to present this in a one-half- to one-page statement of overall strategic goals and maybe one to one and a half pages of operating tactics. You should pay particular attention to the managerial structure of the company; who does what and what will change with the new ownership. Let your guiding philosophy be the immortal words of Will Rogers, "If it ain't broke, don't fix it." It may be that your best plan is to do nothing if you have good in-place managers. Let them do what they do best.

Going to the trouble and expending the effort to develop a good, tight plan does three things. It lets you know what you are buying. It lets the lender know what you are buying. And it keeps you on track. It becomes a master plan for you after you close the deal. The projections become goals and benchmarks by which you can measure your progress. You have these figures on a month-by-month basis for the first year. At the end of that year you should convert those second-year quarterly figures into monthly projections. Continue to use those as goals and benchmarks as you are operating the company through the five-year period.

Most lenders must understand a credit before they can lend to it. Your business plan, as a part of a good financial package, is going to be the document that helps them understand. It must be tight. It must be well structured. It must be clear, straightforward and logical. This kind of presentation increases your credibility as a borrower. It can make up for a lack of actual operating strength. It can make up for a lack of a strong financial statement. The management section should focus on the accomplishments of key managers. This is not a résumé. This is not a biography for a yearbook. It should focus on actual accomplishments and performance in the job. It is a good idea to have a copy of an organization chart so that the lender can get a clear picture of who fits where and does what. This section should also include backup for key managers. I mean, if A is gone, who replaces A when he is on vacation or is out ill?

What are your contingency plans? You should include them. You should include a clear discussion—not lengthy, but complete—of your compensation and incentive program. If you have never prepared one, there are a couple of guidelines provided in the last chapter.

The marketing section of the business plan should answer five main questions. First, what is the product or service being offered? Is it proprietary? Is it protected by patents? Are royalties paid on it? Is it copyrighted? Any drawings or pictures you can include will help communicate it to the lender. Catalogs and brochures might be useful as subsidiary materials.

Second, how is the product priced and how is it positioned in the market? Including a price list can be very useful. You need to address the issue of who determines the pricing. Is the price set by the company or is it set by the competition? Are there one or two major manufacturers who dominate the entire industry and everyone has to price according to their pricing schedule?

Number three, how is the product or service sold in the market? Are you talking about independent reps or do you use an in-house sales force? Do you sell this by direct mail or do you advertise it directly on television with standby operators?

The fourth area of concern is the size of the total market. Within the total market, what share of market does your company have? The concept of market niche may be a new one to you, so let me review it briefly. Within the automobile industry there is a total market of all new cars sold in the United States. But within that overall market there is, for example, a market for station wagons, another for subcompact cars and yet another for convertibles. Each of these can be called a market niche, such as the convertible market niche. What you need to address in your business plan is not just the overall market but the particular niche or niches in which you supply products or services, then what share of those market niches your company has. Earlier I mentioned an analysis of competitors' strengths and weaknesses; the lender is going to be looking for an analysis of competitors within the niche. That is where you are going to look to find the real competition.

The fifth and final issue is new product development and marketing opportunities. What is being done? Is this the kind of company that requires new products every three years because of rapidly changing technology? Are there new marketing opportunities opening up because of the growth of cable television or a change in radio advertising rates? Again, try to put the lender in the picture.

The financial data section must conclude with a system to monitor actual performance against the business plan projections. It must include reports that go back to you, as the new owner, and reports that go to the lender on a monthly basis so that he can monitor the operation. You must detail how corrections will be made if you miss targets. How do you get the company back on track if it begins to drift away? It is a "must" in your plan and it is a "must" for you to do. In business planning, hope for the best, expect the worst and plan for the most likely.

THE FINANCIAL PACKAGE CHECKLIST

1. Historical Financial Statements
2. Pro Forma Financial Statements
3. History and Background of Company
4. Market Analysis
5. Industry Analysis
6. Strategy Statement
7. Financial Plan
8. Biographies of Key Managers
9. Schedules of Major Assets
10. Appraisals
11. Graphs and Photos (optional)

How to Calculate the Equity Kicker

Suppose you have selected the right industry, gone through the analysis and due diligence, picked the right company, structured a good deal and still feel that you lack either the financial capacity or the individual credibility. At this point you should consider putting together a team, perhaps one or two strong advisors whose backgrounds, experience, expertise and connections reinforce those areas in which you feel you are particularly lacking. Or you may want to bring a partner into the deal. This may be the time when you want to go to someone who has a strong financial statement and bring him or her in (or "borrow a statement," as it is called). This person will get some minority interest in the company or other consideration for allowing you to use his or her financial statement to get the deal done.

Lenders are used to seeing someone doing a first LBO with a strong financial partner. They understand that you are going to be doing the legwork on the deal and that the partner is there to provide the financial strength. This will not be an unusual situation to them. It will not stick out. So it is up to you to assess your position in the deal to determine whether you need to bring in one or more good, solid, experienced advisors or perhaps a partner to make it work. In most cases your advisors or partners will expect to participate in the ownership of your deal by taking an equity position. This will be especially true if they have to put cash in the deal. And they will not be the only ones expecting an equity "kicker."

Both the banks and the asset-based lenders are asking for equity kickers as well these days. An equity kicker is a percentage of ownership. It is a deal sweetener. They want a little bit more than just their interest rate return. So they will be asking and you will be saying no. That is part of the negotiations that you go through with the lender. You should expect it.

You may get into a situation where there is a deal that is just so good you know that you have to do it. It should be a deal where all of the numbers work out; it feels right in your gut but you are afraid of losing it unless you can give a little equity. How much equity can you afford to give away? I will show you how you calculate that. Once you consider the possibility of equity kickers there is a third possible source for funding. There are LBO and venture capital funds in virtually every major city in the United

States and many smaller ones. Especially in a case where some equity is needed, the LBO and venture capital funds would be ideal potential partners to approach as the sources of some, but not all, of the financing. You will have to do some careful research to make sure you have the right fund. You are still going to be faced with finding an asset-based lender to take the primary role as the financial source.

Sometimes you need a little of your own money in the deal in order to make it work. Suppose it is a good deal but there are not enough hard assets to provide 100 percent financing. It could be that the seller needs more front-end cash or any number of other reasons. But the bottom line is that there just is not enough cash coming from the assets and cash flow. You know that it is a good business. You know that you can get out with a profit. It is a winner, but you cannot make it work without some money invested on your part. It is not a 100 percent leveraged buyout. To make it work, you need a little bit of equity. That is the time when you consider bringing in an investor partner, someone with whom you are willing to share ownership of your business.

An equity kicker is not a fixed rate of return with a secured position on the assets like a lender's, but a little sweetener to bring an investor into the deal. Where do you go for these sources of equity? Traditionally, friends and family are the first source. Private investors to whom you can get introductions are also good choices. There are a number of leveraged buyout funds where insurance companies, banks, pension funds and other large institutions have invested money with a group of managers specifically for funding LBOs. Normally, they are interested in the larger deals. They rarely get involved in deals that go together with financing much below $5 or $10 million, but you never know until you ask. This is also true of the venture capital funds. There are a number of smaller venture capital funds around that take positions in leveraged buyouts. It has to look good to them. It has to meet their criteria. But if it is a good deal, certainly you would want to take it to them.

If you have done your homework and picked the right funding partner, the chances are high that it will be favorably received even if it is a little bit smaller than the typical deal they get involved in. When equity investors get involved in an LBO they usually put their money into the deal in the form of convertible debt. This is debt that is convertible to equity at some time in the future or after certain conditions have been met.

HOW TO CALCULATE THE EQUITY KICKER

Situation

Purchase Price	$1.5 million
less Asset-based Loans	$1.2 million
Shortfall	$300,000

Equity investor puts up $300,000 as a loan at 13 percent interest secured by a second lien on the assets, but wants an equity kicker. As equity, the return should be in the 20 percent to 35 percent range.

Example

Expected Return on Equity	25%
Actual Return on Second	13%
Shortfall	12%

Twelve percent of $300,000 is $36,000 a year for five years. That comes to $180,000 total shortfall. After fifth year, business is sold for $2 million. Since $180,000 is 9 percent of $2 million, the equity investor must get 9 percent ownership to provide him with enough money upon the sale to cover his projected shortfall in return.

Let me take you through a typical example to see how you would calculate the amount of an equity kicker that your investor partner might expect for getting together with you on your deal. We are going to look at a deal with a purchase price of $1.5 million. Of that $1.5 million, the asset-based lender is going to come up with $1.2 million. You are going to be shy $300,000 in the purchase price. The equity investor is going to put up the $300,000. In this case, assume that he will secure that position with a second lien on the assets. Remember, the asset-based lender has the senior or first position, but there is still a considerable amount of equity left in those assets. In order to satisfy the security concerns of the equity investor, he will take a subordinated or second or junior position on those same assets for his $300,000 at the same rate that the asset-based lender got, which is 13 percent in this case. The $300,000 in the deal as a 13 percent loan is convertible to equity, because it is really equity and deserves an equity return rate. Typically, in LBOs that equity return rate would be 20 percent to 35 percent a year to reflect the greater risk of an equity position than a secured-debt position. For the purposes of this example, I will use a 25 percent return level. The shortfall—which is the difference between the 25 percent that the money should bring and the 13 percent that it is actually earning—is 12 percent per year. On $300,000, that comes to $36,000 a year for five years, or $180,000 over the five-year period.

At the end of five years you sell the business for $2 million. Remember, you bought it for $1,500,000, so you have made a nice profit. The equity kicker is 9 percent of the sale price, since $180,000 is 9 percent of $2,000,000. In other words, for coming in and providing the $300,000 you needed at the time you needed it, in addition to getting a return of 13 percent a year on a second mortgage, that equity investor is going to pick up an upside on the way out of $180,000. That is how you calculate an equity kicker.

7

How to Negotiate the Deal

Successful negotiation is an art. It is not my purpose to turn you into a fully trained professional negotiator. But I am going to give you enough guidelines, rules of thumb and pointers to get you through the negotiations you will need to be able to successfully buy your first LBO. The most important thing for you to remember is that successful negotiation is the art of compromise. Negotiation is not selling. Selling is the art of persuasion. In order to reach a compromise, you need to be able to listen. In order to persuade, you need to be able to talk. These are different skills.

If your negotiations are not fully and completely on a basis of "win-win," you will not be successful in buying your first LBO. By "win-win" I am not talking about some vague idea to which I want you to pay lip service. If there is no way for you to structure a deal so that everyone wins, you are not going to have a deal. You will have put in 300 or 400 hours in a wasted effort. So I would like to give you a little bit of an overview of the negotiation process. Successful negotiation is the heart of a successful deal. Without it, you will simply have an intellectual understanding of how a leveraged buyout works and that is not my purpose. My goal is to get you through your first successful LBO.

Successful negotiating begins with a successful negotiator. That is you. The way in which you begin to be a successful negotiator is to be fully prepared. If there is one single characteristic that singles out and identifies the successful negotiator, it is that he or she is always thoroughly and completely prepared.

When you first contact a potential seller, you will set in motion a dynamic that will last until either the success or failure of the entire negotiation, depending on how you sound, how you look and how you conduct yourself. And so it is very important for you to look and sound and conduct yourself like a successful businessperson. Why is that? Near the end of his play *Pygmalion* (I do not mean the musical comedy *My Fair Lady*) George Bernard Shaw has Eliza Doolittle tell Henry Higgins that the reason she is going to marry Sir Freddy is because when he, Henry Higgins, first met her she was a coal seller's daughter and a coal seller's daughter she would ever be, but when Sir Freddy first met her she was a lady and to him she would always be a lady. And that is called the Pygmalion effect. You are as you first appear to be. No matter what you do subsequent to that first meeting, the impression of you as a serious, credible buyer of that business will remain. You do not get a second chance to create a first impression.

There are books on negotiation that will talk about time of day, who sits where, what to order from the menu. Those are all good things for you to know, but they are only going to give you the forms of successful negotiation. I want you to focus here on the content. I would suggest that you check out a couple of the more popular books, read them and become familiar with the formal techniques because they will aid you. Mornings, particularly between 10:00 A.M. and 11:00 A.M., are usually the best times for these meetings. Right after lunch, 1:00 P.M. to 3:30 P.M., is the worst possible time. It is hardest to get the attention and focus of the potential seller. When you go, remember the importance of that first impression. If you are going to do it right, dress for business: a dark suit, shined shoes, white shirt, conservative tie. A woman would want the ladies' version of the basic business attire. But the most important thing for you is to focus on the overall content of the negotiation process.

I want you to view the entire string of meetings from the first contact until the final document is signed as one continuing stream of events in the negotiating process. And I want you to have an overview of that entire process.

Let us take a look at the early meetings, including that all-important first meeting. Your strategic goal in those early meetings is to put the potential seller at ease. You must become comfortable with him so that you can determine if the right chemistry exists between you, as a potential buyer, and him, as a potential seller, for there to be a deal. You are going to spend several weeks, possibly several months, in negotiating this deal. Once the deal is closed, you are going to spend several more months, possibly a year or two years, with the seller in a "neat and orderly transition." So if you are going to be spending a large amount of time over a year or two with an individual, it would certainly be worth spending a few hours at the beginning to determine whether this is an individual with whom you even want to spend time. Is this an individual whose word you can rely on, whose judgment you can trust? You should know, because you are going to be putting a lot of trust in his word and in his judgment and experience. So be prepared to look him in the eye and see who flinches first.

Some Inside Tips for Success

1. *Visualize Success.* Before you meet, sit in a quiet place, get fully relaxed and visualize the upcoming negotiation session. With your eyes closed, see the prospective seller and yourself going through all the steps of a good, productive meeting. Review each of these tips and imagine how you will use them in your forthcoming session.

2. *Be Prepared.* Success in negotiations belongs to the best-prepared party. Know your facts and figures. Have a firm list of objectives in mind. Have your key questions written down so you do not have to rely on your memory under stress. Develop contingency plans so that you know in advance what you are going to do if your main strategy gets derailed.

3. *Meet Privately.* Pick a quiet, private place to meet. If it is the seller's office, ask permission to close the door. Tell his secretary to hold any calls for you. That will remind the prospect to do likewise. You must make an effort to create an atmosphere that is conducive to good listening.

4. *Be Interested.* Treat every prospective seller as if he were the most interesting speaker in the world. Even if you are bored, even if you think you are going to walk away, listen actively. Remember that everything he says may be useful to you later on, no matter how small it may seem at the time.

5. *Be Relaxed.* Breathe deeply and regularly. Don't forget to breathe when you are nervous or under stress. Let the tension go out of your body without slumping or becoming a rag doll. Remember to help put the seller at ease by mimicking his posture, body language, gestures, vocabulary and speaking rhythms for the first minute or two.

6. *Be Attentive.* As the seller relaxes, face him directly with your arms and legs uncrossed. It may help to lean forward very slightly, but do not give the impression you are just waiting for an opportunity to jump in and speak your piece. Maintain good eye contact and use affirmative nods and expressions. Be careful not to overdo it.

7. *Be Focused.* If the phone rings, the door opens or a parade passes by the window, you must not be distracted. Focus your attention on the seller's words and his underlying intent. Do not forget why you are there.

8. *Be Selective*. You should listen to every word the seller says, but you must listen selectively to hear the key points. Be on the alert for any clues as to his readiness and willingness to sell and what his real needs and concerns are. These are frequently dropped in the middle of seemingly meaningless anecdotes.

9. *Ask Questions*. You are trying to get information. I have suggested several critical questions you must ask. But be sure and probe with follow-up questions. Open-ended questions such as "That's interesting, tell me more" or "What happened then?" usually get good results. They also show that you are listening and that you are interested.

10. *Check Facts*. To make sure you are really understanding what you hear, get some feedback. Restate what the seller has told you, as you understand it, and ask him if you heard it correctly.

11. *Take Notes*. Do not rely on your memory for the important facts and key figures. Take large, obvious notes in plain view. Review your notes after each meeting and use them to summarize and review the previous meeting at each new session.

12. *Retreat If Necessary*. If you get lost or flustered, if you forget some critical question, excuse yourself and go to the rest room. Take a few minutes to get composed, review your list of questions and breathe deeply. Then go back to the negotiations.

13. *Give to Get*. One of the most successful tactics I have ever used in negotiations is "give to get." What it means is that you have to give in on a point before you get the seller to give in on another point. If you think it through, you can manage to give in on a minor point, then have the seller give in on some major point. Remember that all successful negotiations are the result of compromise on both parts.

14. *Handle Anger*. If the seller becomes angry during negotiations, take a break. Take a walk. Tell him you

have to make an important, private call. Anger is a secondary emotion that usually follows fear. So if the seller is angry, you had better find out what he is afraid of and address his concerns directly. If you don't, you will find that you cannot negotiate successfully with an angry seller.

You have found a business and you want to approach the seller. How do you do it? Directly, over the telephone, unless you have a third-party intermediary who can arrange a face-to-face introduction. You do not want that third party or any other member of your team with you, just as you want the seller to come by himself. Where do you set up the meeting? Wherever the seller finds it convenient. If the seller is concerned about confidentiality, he may not want his employees to know he is even meeting with you. He may suggest a nearby restaurant or coffee shop as the site for the first meeting. This makes your job a little more complicated, but accommodate him. Your job here is to win the confidence of the potential seller in the first meeting. It will be the most important event of the deal-making process. That is right. The first meeting between you and the potential seller is the most important event of the deal-making process.

Your primary objective in this meeting is to establish a positive relationship with the seller. The seller is a successful businessman, and businessmen tend to deal with peers. He is not going to sell you his business if he feels you are not potentially his peer. It is absolutely vital that you put him at ease immediately and that you set the pace and tone for the meeting and the entire series of negotiations that will transpire.

How do you make that seller comfortable with you so that you can actually get down to the purposes of that meeting? The most successful way is for you, in the first few minutes you are with the potential seller, to model your body language, your posture and even your tone of voice, vocabulary and word phrasing to reflect his. In other words, you become a mirror to him. The second thing that you should focus on is getting him to talk. Remember, you are the buyer and he is the seller. You want to let him sell you the business. The easiest way for you to do this is to be a good listener. So you are going to have to ask good questions. In the beginning, questions about the history of the business, the seller's involvement, the key moments in the development of the business, main accomplishments of the seller and a walking tour through the business will be the way you can get the seller to open up and become comfortable with you. In that critical first three to five minutes, by simply mirroring back to the seller his own posture, body language and movements, you are going to put him at ease because you are going to convince him subconsciously that you are not a threatening presence in his office. You are, after all, just like him. You are his sort of person.

Your second objective in the first meeting is to establish yourself as a credible buyer who can actually close the deal. You may want to prepare a buyer's package. This is not a résumé, but a simple, brief narrative based on your career that indicates who you are, what you have done, what you are looking for and what you plan to do with it. This is not the place to put your financial statement. But if your financial statement is not strong enough for you to be a credible, potential buyer, you may want to consider teaming up with an individual who is substantial as your partner. You may not actually involve him in any aspect of the deal or the ownership. He may simply be there, with you riding on the coattails of his strong financial statement or his greater experience in business. The seller will perceive you as being the working partner teamed up with a financial partner looking for a deal. It will be clear to the seller that you will be doing the work, you will be in the driver's seat and your partner is there to add credibility to the package. It is not necessary to go so far as to have the package printed, but a clean, neat presentation, professionally typed, of three or four pages can frequently make the difference in your credibility as a first time LBO buyer.

You want to avoid any discussion of price or terms or any exchange of financial statements in the first meeting. Of course, if the seller thrusts his financial statements on you, graciously accept them. More deals are lost because the amateur buyer walks in and says, "What do you want for your business? How do you justify that?" It is foolish to get into an argument over the price without understanding the business. It is your first responsibility to do your due diligence, to analyze the deal, to fully explore the risks and opportunities. Any discussion of value, price or terms is irrelevant until you understand the risks and opportunities.

If the owner, as an amateur seller, is so naive as to ask you, "Well, what are you willing to pay?" you must deflect the question with the response that you simply do not know because you have not analyzed the business. You have a hidden agenda here. You are attempting to find out, in the course of this meeting, whether the seller is a real seller. Is he really ready to close a deal? Are there assets there that are financeable? Your hidden agenda is to also show that you are financially capable, operationally able and personally honest, because the seller will not want to do business with a potential buyer whose credibility, capability or honesty he suspects for even a moment. I have seen several cases where a seller sold his business at a lower price to a buyer he liked rather than take a higher price from a potential buyer that he distrusted.

You must carefully qualify the seller because seller's remorse can be a real problem. You can put hundreds of hours into a deal and find that, at the last minute, when it comes right down to the close and it is time for the seller to put his name on the bottom line, he has a change of heart. Seller's remorse grips him. He just cannot go through with the deal. And you have months of time go right down the drain. I watched a five-month effort that my wife and I had mounted to sell our third business come to a complete halt because, at the last minute, she got seller's remorse and held out for a higher price. It took us another six months to get that same buyer back to the table at exactly the same price and terms. Only now we were six months more tired and burned out than we were when we started. Seller's remorse is real. It can be a costly problem for you as a first-time buyer.

How Do You Qualify a Seller?

Well, the main thing you are interested in is, does he have a real motive to sell his business? Does he have a timetable? I have already indicated that the primary reason that sellers sell good businesses is boredom or burnout. They are tired of doing the same thing day in and day out. They want out. Whether they want to go on to another challenge or retire is really irrelevant. It is difficult, perhaps impossible, for them to be as succinct as those words— *bored*, *burned out*—but you can tell if you are dealing with a bored or burned-out seller. If you are talking about an individual who is fifty-five to sixty-five years old, it only takes one or two questions to probe the issues of health or age. I have had potential sellers even volunteer the fact that all of their friends have had triple bypass operations. You know what their primary concern is then. They know they are not immortal. They see what is happening to their friends. They read the obituaries. They are concerned. They are developing a real motive to sell their business.

One or two questions can surface the issue of a family successor. Is there a son or daughter who is going to take over the business? Is that niece or nephew out on the production line going to move into the front office? It does not take much to find out, but you must determine whether there is a real motive. Are you dealing with a divorce or partnership-dissolution situation? Does the seller have estate planning considerations or other financial concerns? Is he trying to diversify his asset holdings?

What kinds of questions am I talking about? Simple, direct questions such as "Have you made any plans for retirement?" and "Why have you been thinking about selling your business?" And notice I suggest "thinking about." Do not put him on the spot or make him feel uncomfortable. Do not ask him, "Why are you selling your business?" It will make him nervous if he has only recently come to the emotional decision and still has not fully rationalized it in his mind. It is much gentler, much more effective, to approach him with the question "Why have you been thinking about selling your business?"

Another effective question you should ask is "If you sell, what will you miss most about the business?" Here you are going to begin to surface the issues that will become your bargaining chips in later negotiations. The seller will begin to tell you exactly, point by point, those things that he will miss the most about his business. Is it the country club membership? Is he going to miss a new Mercedes or Cadillac every year? Is it his health insurance program or his key-man life insurance? Which of his perks is he truly going to regret giving up when he thinks about selling his business? These are going to become the bargaining chips with which you are going to buy his business, so you might as well let him give you those chips in the first meeting.

A key question you must ask is "What do you plan to do with the proceeds of a sale?" You will find the rare potential seller who will not answer that question. He will feel that it is none of your business. Fine. You do not need to deal with that person. You are making a perfectly reasonable request. After all, you are going to put a very large sum of money in his hands. It could be as much as $1 million to $5 million. You have a normal, natural businessman's interest in the answer to the question "What do you plan to do with the proceeds of a sale?" If he won't answer, walk away. Again, you are looking for bargaining chips. If he says that he is going to invest it here or there, or he does not really need it all right now, he is giving you information that you can use to help structure your leveraged buyout offer.

In this first meeting, you are trying to put him at ease. I have found that one of the quickest ways to put someone at ease is to get him talking about a subject with which he is very familiar. After all, he has spent twenty years with the business. He is very familiar with it, so get him to open up with "And how did you happen to get started in this business?" He may go all the way back to his grandfather in the First World War, and you may have to sit and listen for two or three hours. Do it. The longer he talks, the more he is telling you about that business, and the more comfortable he is feeling with you. By the end of that time, he is going to think you are actually a pretty good person. You sat there and listened to him talk for hours about his favorite subject, and you never said a word.

Another question you do not want to overlook is "What has been your most important decision here?" You should follow that one with "What have been the biggest problems you have encountered building this company to its present size?" Then you should ask "How could new working capital best be used in the company?" All of these questions will tend to elicit key concerns in the mind of the seller. The answers will tell you the areas that you should pay particular attention to as you analyze the deal in doing your due diligence.

A final item on your agenda in this first meeting will be the walk-through or plant tour. You want the seller to take you through the premises, have him show you around. If there is real estate involved in the deal, you want to take a look at what condition it is in. How old is it? How much of it is there really? What kind of access does it have? You may want to ask a question about any mortgage due. Is it free and clear? Pay particular attention to the fixtures, machinery, equipment and inventory, They will tell their own story if you let them. Are they beat up? Do they look as if they have been neglected or are in need of repair? Are they dirty? Is the inventory gathering dust in the corners? Is it neat, well organized? What kind of an operation are you dealing with?

Avoid any controversial subjects. Remember, your role at this meeting is to listen. He is the seller. He is selling you his business. You are the buyer. Simply listen and ask the questions. Do not get into arguments over how much anything is worth. Avoid all discussions of price at this point. If he should point out a piece of equipment and tell you that it is worth ten times what he is carrying it for on his books, nod your head and take notes. Remember, you are there to make a good contact with him. Remain objective throughout the situation. Do not make judgments. When you have concluded the tour, set a time for your next meeting, usually no sooner than a week and no later than two weeks. Review the materials you have gathered and prepare for subsequent negotiations. If you have decided not to do the deal, this is the time to say no.

It is very likely, with the amount of material you have to cover and the number of meetings you have, that you will get into the habit of taking notes. You do not want to be threatening to the seller. If you are going to take notes, take them on a large pad of paper; the lined, yellow, legal-size pad works out very well. Take notes in large writing with black ink on top of his desk or out in the open. Taking small, cribbed notes on small notepads that you hide in your pocket or purse is not a good idea. It increases the level of the seller's paranoia that you are somehow stealing his business secrets. Do not under any circumstances take a tape recorder. Nothing can have a more chilling effect on a free, frank, open discussion than the appearance of a tape recorder. No one wants to go that far on the record in an initial meeting. So leave the tape recorder at home. If you feel that you absolutely have to get away to write down something or to check your notes, excuse yourself and go to the rest room. You can use that time to review the questions so that when you come back to the session you can pick up and not miss any of these key questions. The issues involved here are far too important to stand on propriety. Being prepared is the hallmark of the successful negotiator. Do what you have to do to get through these sessions. Your strategic goal in these early meetings is to develop a warm, comfortable relationship with the seller. As soon as you introduce the subject of price and terms, the entire nature of the relationship changes and the clock starts to run. You introduce an element of adversarial relationship. The seller knows that you have got his money in your pocket and he will begin to pressure you in order to get it out. If it becomes necessary to deal with the seller's direct questions—"How much were you thinking of paying?" or "I've been thinking of asking $2 million. What do you think about that?"—your only response can be to deflect with such answers as "Based on what I've seen so far that seems a reasonable amount" or "Until I completely understand the risks and opportunities involved here, I think any discussion of price and terms is premature."

What do you do about the seller who demands that you give him a copy of your financial statement? My suggestion is that in the course of your preparation you contact two or three potential leaders, one of whom should be willing to give you a conditional letter of commitment. This letter usually states that if any deal you bring him is as you have represented and the assets are at the values you have stated, the lender will provide the financing for you to do the deal. Normally, this will satisfy the seller's curiosity as to whether he is dealing with a substantial, reliable and potentially effective buyer. On this matter of financial statements, do not in these early meetings get into a position where you are asking the seller for his financial statements. You are trying to get ballpark figures by asking general questions. If you put pressure on the seller to get copies of his financial statements in these early meetings, you may find yourself in an uncomfortable position.

It is not until you move into the middle portion of the meetings that your purpose is to get information. This is the time when you need to see the seller's financials. By this point, you will have had a meeting or two and a couple of telephone calls. You may have spent as much as eight or ten hours together. You are now into the middle portion of the negotiations. You will want to be in control of the pace of the negotiations as you move along. Meetings should be spaced at about one- to two-week intervals. If you meet more often than once a week, you are going to give the impression of being too anxious. If you meet less frequently than every two weeks, you are going to give the impression that you really do not care that much about the deal. It is a very delicate matter of balance. I leave the final decision up to you, but those are my guidelines.

During these middle meetings, if you have followed you due diligence checklist in the Appendix, you will see that there is a considerable amount of information you need to get from this seller. You must pose these questions in a nonthreatening way. For example, if you ask the seller for a list of his key accounts, you are going to make him very nervous. However, if you tell him that you would like to take a look at his accounts receivable aging analysis, he is going to be less threatened even though it amounts to the same thing. The accounts receivable are a list of the amounts of money owed to the company by key customers. The same is true with regard to suppliers. If you were to ask the seller for a list of the company's key suppliers, you would encounter the same kind of resistance. However, if you ask, in an offhand manner, for a copy of the accounts payable aging analysis, you will have a list of the key suppliers, and you will not have upset the seller.

Competition is frequently a subject about which a potential seller has difficulty providing accurate information. It is going to be necessary for you to dig in order to get the kind of information you need to prepare a competitive analysis that will satisfy you and any lender that might be involved in the deal.

When you begin your organizational analysis to get a picture of the managerial structure of the company, you need to involve the seller to get a clear picture. The chances are that he is not going to have his organizational chart on paper already, so you are going to have to get him to help you draw the picture of the company. You can do this by asking him to go through all of his key employees name by name. You must ask him the name of the employee, how long the employee has been with the company, how much the employee earns, and whether or not, in his opinion, that employee is going to stay on after he sells the company. You really do not care what his opinion is as to whether or not the employee is going to stay on after the seller has sold his company. It is impossible for him to say really. He is certainly not going to guarantee it. The whole point of asking this question is for you to continually repeat the phrase to him, "How long will they stay on after you have sold the company"—"after you have sold the company"—"after you have sold the company." The point of this repetition is a nearly hypnotic way to get the seller conditioned to the notion that he is selling his company. Anything you can do to make him more comfortable with this notion is going to further your cause and make the negotiations easier when you get down to the final meetings.

The final concern you are going to have about this middle group of meetings is the actual financial structure of the company itself. You should have made general notes when you went through the business. You should have added to your knowledge in subsequent meetings as the seller told you about the visible assets, the inventory and the hidden assets of the company that are not reflected in the books. At this point you are going to ask him to get very, very specific about the total amount and form of his compensation and the compensation of family members and close friends who are associated with the company. You will look not only at salary but also at interest-free loans and all of his other perks, anything that he took out of the company in the form of compensation. Do not overlook outside consulting income that came to him as the owner of the company. You are trying to get a complete picture of what the seller was getting so you can do your rescheduled income statement. He is going to be the source of that information. So when you do the financial analysis, look for the true value of assets, not the book value reported on the financial statement. Look for the hidden assets, the ones that are not even carried on the books. You want to take a look at the asset account, which is a listing of the dates and amounts at which the various assets were purchased. Many of them may have already been written off and would represent hidden assets. Before you get through the middle set of meetings, remember to get all the information you need on the sales and marketing component, the organizational and management component and the financial component. When you have finished you should have the information you need.

You are now going to let some time pass, because you have to do a lot of homework. It would not be unusual for you to spend a couple of weeks analyzing, researching, checking out and structuring the deal that you come back and offer him at the final meeting. You should give yourself about two weeks to get all of this done. Where your strategic objective in the early meetings was to get comfortable and in the middle meetings it was to get the information, your objective in the last meeting is to get the deal done. Now you are going to introduce the subject of terms and price. You always begin with terms and then go into price. Somewhere along the line you will have, in the course of your conversation, developed an idea of what that seller is expecting. For example, you know that he is thinking about a nice, round $2 million. Your response to that has been

"Well, based on what I know so far, that sounds like a reasonable price." Your reason for doing this is that you want the seller to get used to the idea of being a millionaire. The truth is that the fear of loss is a far more powerful motivator than the promise of gain. If that seller over a period of six weeks or two months has become used to thinking of himself as getting $2 million for the sale of his business and if he senses that he is losing you, then he is going to be far more flexible when it comes to the final negotiations. So you have to let him think that $2 million is a perfectly fine price. You have been careful not to contradict him. You have not argued with him. You did not make the amateur's mistake of saying, "That's too much."

You know what he wants and needs because you have already asked him in the early meetings. That was the whole point of those questions qualifying the seller and determining his real wants and needs. And now you have structured a deal to meet those needs. A primary component of it, in most cases, will be a big, fat perk package. In most deals you have a 25 percent cash down payment and the balance to be financed over a three- to seven-year term.

You begin your final meeting by presenting an offer. You are going to emphasize, point by point, the contents of your written offer, beginning with the terms. The terms you are going to begin with are the perks, not the down payment. State clearly each and every perk that is a part of your offer. Say, "I am going to continue your country club membership at $10,000 a year for 5 years; that's $50,000. Is that acceptable?" Be sure you get his agreement on each item as you mention it. "I am going to continue your attendance at the annual industry convention in Bermuda at a cost of $4,000 per year for five years for a total of $20,000. Is that acceptable to you?" You are going to go through, naming each perk as you go. Never, never understate the benefits by lumping them together. That is what you are giving him. You are getting him to accept the benefits. You do it by repeating them and making them attractive. Once he has agreed to each and every term of the deal, including the cash down payment of 25 percent and the term payments, you will see that the price itself will fall out as a logical by-product. Remember, when you valued the business, you gave yourself a range. Now you have structured that range in such a way that you are limiting your negotiations to the fine tuning. Perhaps a compromise in the middle of the range will end up being the final purchase price. So begin with the terms and get agreement to each and every term. By fully stating each term as a benefit, you make it very clear to the seller that if he says no, he realizes what he is giving up. You can back him into accepting the final, logical conclusion, which is your purchase price. Once that happens, you have done your deal.

If the seller resists at any point along the way, one of two things has happened. Either you did not properly qualify him as a real, motivated seller, or you have not asked the right questions to get at his real needs. Stop at the point of resistance and ask directly, "What's wrong? Where did I lose you? I thought you wanted to keep your country club membership. Talk to me. What do you really want out of this deal?"

If price is the seller's only consideration, the chances are he is not really a motivated seller. Take your excess earnings calculations out of your file and go over the forms with him step by step to share your thinking with him. He may point out some error in your approach or he may see where he was being unreasonable.

It can strengthen your positon if you compare the profit from the business to the return on a safe investment like T-bills. At the time I bought Sam's business, the recast net profit ($270,000) represented an annual return of 17.5 percent on my investment (the $1,550,000 purchase price) at a time when safe investments were yielding over 10 percent. If Sam had held out for a $2 million price, the return would have gone down to 13.5 percent. This rate of return would not have justified the risk involved in making a $2 million investment—even if it was not my money that was invested.

Once you have educated the seller by going through the steps to arrive at a realistic price range and you have compared the return available to you in his business to a safe alternative investment, you should have a deal. Or you don't have a real seller. If he is not a real seller, walk away. Go on to your next deal.

If the seller accepts your terms and you agree on a price, you should have a written letter of intent for you both to sign. You should have brought two copies, one for each of you to keep after you have both signed both copies. There is a sample letter of intent in the next chapter, but you should have your attorney prepare or thoroughly review your own for each deal. Once you have the signed letter of intent, you are ready to open a trust security account and close your deal.

8

How to Close the Deal

A smile and a handshake may close the deal, but it is the paperwork that makes it real. Let's look at how you close the deal properly. You must make sure that after you have done all of this work and successfully negotiated a deal you want that you actually dot all the *i*'s and cross all the *t*'s properly to make sure that the deal stays done. This means that you must pay attention to the documentation that goes along with every deal from beginning to end.

The first document you are likely to encounter is a confidentiality agreement. If you are going to run into a confidentiality agreement, the need for it will be raised by the seller, usually at the beginning of the negotiation process. It will not happen in every deal. Not every seller is going to be paranoid enough to require you to sign a nondisclosure or nonuse confidentiality agreement. But you will find sellers who are afraid to open up their innermost secrets, their real books and records, and share them with you, a perfect stranger. In order to make this type of seller feel comfortable so you can get into the real due diligence of the deal, it will be necessary for such an agreement to be signed.

To avoid any problems, you should be prepared with a document of your own. You should come with a letter of nonproprietary interest in your pocket or briefcase. This will relieve you of the need to sign his letter. Basically your letter should say, "I do not want you to tell me anything secret just yet." With this kind of letter you can get through the early meetings without arousing too much fear in the seller. At the same time you will not be exposing yourself to unnecessary risk. From your point of view, you have selected an industry and you are going to be spending a considerable amount of time looking at ten or fifteen businesses within that industry. You do not want to preclude yourself from either finding information or using that information by signing a nondisclosure or nonuse agreement. If you are dealing with a business in which true trade secrets or proprietary information are involved, and you have concluded the early round of negotiation meetings and are going to do some real due diligence, it is appropriate for you to sign such an agreement. Make sure that your attorney drafts it or at least reviews the one offered by the seller.

The next document that you will be likely to encounter is a letter of intent. This usually occurs during the final stage of negotiations at the last meeting when you actually get agreement on terms and price. You should present your letter of intent in person to the seller. It should spell out in writing the terms and price that you are ready to pay for this business. If it is necessary, as a result of your final round of negotiations, to change some aspect of the deal, then you should make the change on the face of the letter of intent. You should initial the change and have the seller initial it. If it is a multipage letter, both of you should initial each page. This is the way to handle situations when you and the seller really do agree but there is some minor variation or modification that the seller wants in order to feel perfectly comfortable with the deal.

In addition to terms and price, a central point you must address in your letter of intent is whether you intend to acquire the seller's company itself (assuming that he is the owner of 100 percent of the stock in the company) or whether you are purchasing only the assets of the company. In this sense, at the time of the sale, the assets of the company can be anything that the buyer and seller agree upon, including the name of the company and its cash. The term "asset" is not limited in its use to the assets I described in the analysis of the balance sheet, but anything that the buyer and seller agree upon are assets of the business. Personally, I prefer the "assets only" approach when buying a business (the IRS Section 337 approach).

In the first place, when you purchase just the assets of the seller, including the name of his company, you are limiting your liability. Even though the seller intends to be fair and honest with you, he cannot know about every potential liability he may have. Your interest is in acquiring the assets and the opportunity of the business, not lawsuits that you do not know about. The fact is that the seller may not even know about them. If someone slipped on the seller's sidewalk two weeks ago and is only now thinking about suing him for his bad back, the seller is not going to be able to tell you. It may end up coming back to haunt you. This is particularly true in this particular era of excessive litigation over environmental concerns, hazardous wastes and product liabilities. I would advise you to limit your liability by doing assets-only transactions.

Practically speaking, it is difficult for you, as a buyer, to escape complete and total liability. The courts have permitted certain unsecured creditors to sue the new corporation that you would form in order to avoid the liability regardless of the structure of the deal that you have put together. And particularly in California, product liability lawsuits have been filed in courts and the courts have allowed them to proceed against the new company. At the very least you should attempt to limit your liability by acquiring only the assets of the company and forming a new corporation that will assume the name of the old corporation.

When the seller sells you his assets for cash or notes, under IRS Section 337 the corporation that is doing the selling pays no tax if it is liquidated within one year and the total value of the deal is under $10 million. This means that the seller is only taxed as an individual. However, this "window" is going to be closed by the new tax law (the Tax Reform Act of 1986). After December 31, 1988, this will no longer be a tax-free transaction. The corporation, if it is liquidated within a year, pays no tax, with the possible exception of recapture of depreciation and investment tax credits. Now, those are a couple of very interesting issues. If the corporation has been depreciating its assets for tax purposes at an accelerated rate that is greater than the rate it has been using on its books, then the seller owes the IRS tax and penalties on the difference between the greater and lesser depreciation. That money is due immediately after the sale, regardless of when the seller receives money for those assets. This can be an issue, especially if the total cash consideration is higher than the book value of the assets. This is an issue you should be aware of because it will figure into the seller's tax planning for the closing. And you should be prepared to accommodate him as long as it does not damage your deal structure.

I would also advise you to avoid what are called Section 369 "tax-loss carry-forward" deals for a couple of reasons. First, the only real way you can take advantage of a tax-loss carry-forward is if you are involved in the purchase of the stock of the corporation that has the tax loss to carry forward. The second reason is that under the current rules and regulations the climate for these deals is very risky. Keep in mind that you are looking to buy a successful company. You are not going to find many successful companies with substantial operating losses to carry forward. So it is probably not going to be an issue. If you think that the advantage of a deal is a large tax loss to carry forward to cover your profits in the years ahead, think again. My advice would be to forget it.

Always form a new corporation into which the assets you are buying will be put. It is neater, cleaner and safer to deal with each one of your LBO acquisitions as an individual entity. Do not try to make do with some other proprietorship, partnership, or existing corporation that you have already set up. Start from ground zero. Do not try to save the $200 or $300 it will cost you to form the new corporation. It just is not worth it.

Be prepared for the deal to fall apart two or three times, perhaps more, before it closes. The risks are great between the time you and the seller reach agreement at the end of negotiations and the time you actually have your deal put to bed, where papers are signed and money changes hands. A deal is not a deal until the money is in the bank. So do be prepared to see it fall apart and require more negotiations, because you are now going to have other parties involved intensely. The seller is going to have his attorney and perhaps his accountant. You are going to have your attorney and your accountant involved. There will also be some appraisers and possibly a lender or two in the deal. When you increase the number of players arithmetically, the number of potential deal-breaking points increases geometrically.

I have included a copy of the letter of intent I used to buy Sam's business for you to look over. This is a straight assets-only deal with a $350,000 cash down payment and deferred payments of $1,050,000, plus a five-year perk package worth $150,000. I suggest that you use the type of hold-back or reserve clause that I did in item number 5. By having Sam leave me with $100,000 for a year, I gave myself some real protection against undisclosed liabilities and bad accounts. I also got to use Sam's cash as working capital for one year at a very nice rate. No bank would have lent me that kind of money on a business that was a complete LBO. Needless to say, I had none of my own money in this deal.

SAMPLE LETTER OF INTENT

March 13, 1986

Sam F. Sulik
Samco, Inc.
Cleveland, Ohio

Dear Sam:

This letter is to set forth the understanding and agreements reached between you, as the Seller, and me, as the Buyer, regarding my purchase of all of the assets and liabilities of Samco, Inc. Here are the details of our agreement.

1. *Assets Purchased.* Buyer will purchase from Seller all of the assets of Samco, Inc., of every kind and nature, real, personal or intangible, as set forth in the financial statements of December 31, 1985, or since or hereafter acquired by or disposed of by the Seller in the ordinary course of business. The Seller agrees to maintain all of the assets of the business in their present condition and to inform Buyer in advance of any intended purchase, sale or material change until the time of closing. Buyer is not purchasing the common stock of Seller's corporation.

2. *Assumption of Liabilities.* Buyer will assume, acquire and be fully responsible for all liabilities of Seller as set forth in the financial statements of December 31, 1985, or which have arisen, been discharged, or otherwise modified in the ordinary course of business since that date. The Seller agrees to incur no extraordinary liabilities without informing the Buyer in advance of Seller's intention. Buyer will not assume any liability not disclosed by Seller in the financial statements or in the definitive agreement of terms and conditions of the proposed purchase and sale.

3. *Purchase Price.* At the closing, Buyer will pay to Seller for all assets purchased and a covenant not to compete, $350,000 cash as a down payment and will execute a promissory note for $350,000 with monthly payments of $458.33 for twenty (20)

157

years on an amortized basis, and Buyer will execute a promissory note for $700,000 due and payable in one payment twenty (20) years from date of closing, both notes secured by a subordinated, junior lien on the assets of the business or by a guarantee from an independent third party acceptable to Seller, and Buyer will enter the employment agreement with Seller described below.

4. *Employment Agreement.* At the closing, Buyer will enter into a five-year employment agreement with Sam F. Sulik providing for medical, dental and life insurance for five years up to a maximum of $10,000 per year in premiums, plus Buyer will sell to Seller the 1985 Mercedes-Benz currently used by Seller for $1 (present fair market value: $40,000) and provide auto insurance, registration fees, repairs, gas, oil, tires and other automobile operating expenses for five years up to a maximum of $6,000 per year and salary of $6,000 per year to Sam F. Sulik for five years, for a total consideration of $150,000.

5. *Reserve.* Seller agrees to leave $100,000 in cash from the down payment on deposit with the Buyer for a period of twelve (12) months from the closing as a reserve against undisclosed liabilities or uncollectable accounts receivable. Buyer agrees to pay Seller simple interest on this reserve deposit at the rate of nine percent (9%) per annum in monthly installments of $750 and to refund the entire balance if no undisclosed claims have been substantiated and if all accounts receivable have been collected, allowing for a bad debt write-off equal to that experienced by the business during the past three calendar years.

6. *Indemnification.* Seller agrees to indemnify and hold harmless Buyer and his agents, employees and affiliates, from any claims, cost, expense or liability asserted against any of the indemnified parties based on any liability of or created by Seller at any time before or after the closing.

7. *Binding Effect & Condition.* This agreement in principle is intended to be a binding obligation of Buyer and Seller, subject to the conditions set forth above and includes the following:

a. The execution of a definitive agreement on terms and conditions mutually satisfactory to Buyer and Seller and containing representations, warranties, conditions and covenants appropriate for a transaction of the type set forth in this agreement. Buyer and Seller agree to use their best efforts to negotiate and execute a definitive agreement as soon as practicable hereafter.

b. Receipt of approvals, if required, of any governmental regulatory authorities.

c. The continued operation of the ordinary business of Samco, Inc. without changes in the number of employees, the nature or amount of their compensation, the purchase, sale or encumbrance of assets, the assumption of liabilities or any other change in the business as Seller has represented it to Buyer or as set forth in the financial statements of December 31, 1985.

8. *Broker Fees*. Neither Seller nor Buyer has retained any broker in connection with this transaction.

9. *Miscellaneous*. This agreement shall be construed under and governed by the laws of the State of Ohio. Any disputes under this agreement that cannot be resolved by the parties shall be referred to arbitration proceedings in accordance with the rules and regulations of the American Arbitration Association.

10. *Expiration of Offer*. This offer expires unless signed and accepted by the Buyer and Seller at midnight Monday, March 17, 1986.

If this letter sets forth your understanding of our agreement, please sign and date it in the space below.

Sincerely,

_____
Lionel Haines, Buyer   Date

Agreed and Accepted:

_____
Sam F. Sulik, Seller   Date

Some other issues you are going to want to keep in mind in terms of documentation as you go along are employee confidentiality agreements and written personnel policies. When you have formed your new corporation and the deal is closing, have all employees of the seller's corporation sign confidentiality agreements that will cover them as employees of the new corporation. You also need written personnel policies and procedures. Do not be the entrepreneur who ends up having an off–balance sheet liability because you did not have a written use-it-or-lose-it policy for vacations and paid sick leave or anything else that opens you up to a similar liability. Start out right by making sure that you dot all the *i*'s and cross all the *t*'s from the beginning. The time to do that is when those new employees come on board.

You will also have to have a trust security agreement and instructions prepared by your attorney. The trust security agreement sets up the escrow account into which the deal is going to close. You may find some resistance to the idea of using a trust security account as long as the deal is going to close under the provisions of the Uniform Commercial Code, particularly the Bulk Sales Act, which is Section 6 of the code. However, you want to insist on it for your protection. You should go into this with a belt and suspenders. You need to be doubly safe and protected. So be sure to have a trust security agreement and instructions drafted by your attorney to cover exactly what you intend to do.

The final set of documents that is going to be prepared in the transaction is the purchase and sale agreement with its related documentation. These should always be prepared by your attorney. Do no try to save the extra bucks that it is going to cost by having the seller's attorney prepare this very crucial, vital documentation. It should always be done by your attorney in consultation with your CPA.

Your attorney has to recognize and be aware of the

needs of the seller's attorney. If your attorney does not satisfy the seller's attorney's needs, then you are going to find that the seller's attorney will act as a roadblock or possible deal breaker. It is up to you to monitor the performance of your attorney. Make sure that he is communicating with the seller's attorney, so that when you get to the actual closing the seller's attorney is your ally working toward the closing of the deal. After all, if he has been the attorney for the seller's corporation, this deal means that he will be losing a good client. You have to motivate him and work with him in order to get him to work with you at the closing.

To put this into a time perspective, take a look at the sequence of events from the point at which you conclude negotiations and have your agreement on terms and price. The first thing you will have prepared and signed is the final letter of intent. This includes your intention to buy and the seller's intention to sell the assets of the company for a specific price on specific terms. It can be a simple, one-page letter or it can run two or three pages. It should be prepared by your attorney.

Once that letter of intent is signed, a number of responsibilities fall on your shoulders. Serious, final due diligence is the first of these. You may want to have your CPA come in and do a businessman's review. Certainly he will help you in analyzing the books and records to make sure that you have surfaced all of the critical issues in terms of the assets, liabilities and other areas of concern in the deal. You may also be busy preparing a financing package and making a final selection of a lender. As you have gone along in this deal you have identified some potential key players such as the lender. Now you are going to make a final selection because you have a real deal to take to them for consideration.

Next you are going to negotiate and prepare the definitive purchase agreement. Here again, your attorney is going to prepare the purchase agreement for you using the terms and conditions of the letter of intent as the guideline. You are also going to be forming a new corporation. And, as the board of directors of your new corporation, you must adopt an official resolution approving the purchase of the seller's assets by your new corporation. The seller's board of directors has to approve the sale of assets subject to the approval of the seller as the shareholders. This may sound like a ridiculous situation if the seller is the president of the corporation as well as the board of directors and the sole shareholder, but he actually has to go through the formal, legal proceeding. Remember, the point of this documentation is to get it right and make sure that every *i* is dotted and every *t* is crossed.

The next thing that happens is that your attorney files the required notices under the Uniform Commercial Code for the Bulk Sales Act compliance. And you are ready for the closing. At the closing there will be a final purchase agreement as well as a bill of sale and an assignment from the seller to the buyer. This covers basically what is coming from him to you. The cash money and promissory notes are going from you to him. When that happens, the deal is closed.

Be sure to have your attorney check with the secretary of state's office at the close of business the day before the deal closes for any last-minute liens recorded against the assets. Then make sure that you have the closing at 9:00 A.M. the next morning. This will prevent any last-minute slipups, anybody coming in and filing some kind of an action against the corporation at the last minute that might in any way cloud your title to those assets. You want to be doubly certain. Your attorney will have checked earlier in his due diligence. Your attorney will have given you a letter stating that there is no litigation pending or no undisclosed claims on the assets. But you want him to call the day before you close just to be sure.

There will be other closing documents in addition to the purchase and sale agreement. There will be exhibits.

Typically, there will be copies of the promissory notes to be signed, the final balance sheet of the company, any contracts that must be honored by you in your new corporation, title to any property involved, and any patents or trademarks that might be involved in the transfer. There should also be a list of any litigation pending or actually ongoing at the time of the sale. In addition, there should be a letter of opinion from the seller's attorney and a letter of opinion from your attorney saying that all the terms and provisions of the agreement have been met. This puts them on written record and makes them liable. That is why you insist on having both of those letters there. In this way you have recourse, and so does the seller, to the attorneys if the deal begins to fall apart because the documentation was not put together properly.

There will also be the actual promissory note or notes involved and whatever security agreements are going to be involved. Remember, I mentioned senior debt and subordinated debt. Both of those are going to have to be documented with security agreements if they have been used. Then there will be any bills of sale or deeds (if there is real estate involved), a notice of assumption of liabilities, and copies of the resolutions of the boards of directors from the buyer's corporation and the seller's corporation approving the purchase and sale of the assets. If there are vehicles involved, there will be additional bills of sale and vehicle agreements attached. There should also be funding instructions that say who gets what when which conditions are met.

The centerpiece, the central focus of the documentation, will be the purchase and sale agreement itself. I would like to highlight some of the contents of a typical purchase and sale agreement, not because I want you to be prepared to be your own attorney, but because you should know what to look for when you review this document.

• One of the first things you should come across are the representations, or "rep" for short, and warranties of the company, the seller and the buyer. Under the seller's and the company's representations and warranties I want you to pay particular attention to undisclosed liabilities. The seller should represent to you that there are no undisclosed liabilities. If they have been previously undisclosed, at this point they are going to disclose them to you. This would also cover any pending litigation about which you have no knowledge. The seller provides you with a list of any litigation that has been filed. Here he is saying that there is no additional litigation.

• There should also be a representation covering conflicts of interest. You want to know if the seller or anyone involved in the selling corporation has an interest of 5 percent or more in any other corporation, especially if it is either a customer of the seller's corporation or a supplier to the seller's corporation. You want to know all about any hidden conflicts of interest.

• There will be a section on the conduct of the business pending the transfer. You do not want the seller to go out and give everybody a 5 percent raise just before you take over the business because he feels guilty about selling. This provision makes sure that the seller is put on notice that he is not to make any material change in the way that he has been conducting the business. You should also have covered this point in the letter of intent.

• There will be a section on conditions precedent to the obligations of the buyer and also the seller and his company. Review them and make sure that you understand that the conditions must be met before the obligations are assumed.

• There will then be a section on indemnification and resolution of disputes. One of the paragraphs in that section will be on misrepresentations. It is under the provisions of that paragraph on misrepresentations that the seller will be obligated to pay for any appraisals that were made or audits that were conducted if the seller has misrepresented the nature, extent or value of the assets.

• You will also want to have an arbitration provision in the resolution of disputes as opposed to a provision requiring lawsuits. It is a lot cheaper. There may be some drawbacks to arbitration, but it is faster and easier for you in the long run.

• You should also have a section dealing with termination and abandonment. You have already made a commitment to the deal, so you are not concerned about walking away. You should have your attorney set up provisions that allow you to get out if there is any fraud, misrepresentation, or if you are not able to complete the financing. What you are trying to do here is make it costly for the seller if he does not close the deal. What it should say here is that the seller agrees to pay you, as liquidated damages and not as a penalty, some sum of money if he backs out. I suggest that you make it a substantial sum of money, such as $100,000 to $200,000 in a $500,000 to $5 million deal. This should help prevent seller's remorse. If the seller does not want to close, it should cost him money because you have put a lot of time into this deal. That is what termination and abandonment is about.

• You want to make sure that there are sections on the covenants not to compete, the trades act secrets portion and the employment agreement, if you are using that in your deal structuring.

• There will also be a section on brokerage. This is where the various fees get paid if you are using a broker. This is also where your appraisal fees get paid and where your financing fees get paid. The section on brokerage fees recognizes and states who gets what fees.

That is pretty much it as far as the purchase and sale agreement is concerned. Those are the key issues. You should go over all the documentation with your attorney and make sure that you are adequately covered. When you are talking to your attorney, tell him what it is that you want to do. When he has done it you want to ask him, "Have I accomplished what I want to do? Is there anything else I need to do in order to adequately protect myself?'' He is working for you. He is going to take a lot of the burden off your shoulders. I do not want you to play at being your own attorney, but do work with your attorney properly. He is providing a professional service for you. If you remember to ask those two questions, you will find that you can work with him effectively as you move through the proper closing of the deal.

9

How to Survive Your First Year

Congratulations! You have bought yourself a good, successful business using none of your own money. You have followed the system step by step. You went through all of the details, negotiated the deal successfully and closed it properly. Now, here you are, the first day in your new business. It is your baby now. What do you do with it? That moment you take over can be pretty frightening unless you are prepared.

The first thing I suggest you do is to meet with the employees. You should meet with them individually. You should organize the schedule of meetings by seniority and dollars of salary. You should start at the top, with those people who have been there the longest and who make the most money. You should work your way down until you have been through a face-to-face meeting with every employee. Obviously, there are going to be some key employees, those who have been there for a long time or are pulling down fairly healthy salaries. You need to meet with them for longer periods of time by making your session special, such as taking them out for lunch or dinner. But you must do this as soon as you can. I mean from day one for you in the business.

You are going to probe them with questions such as "What would you do if you owned this company?" or "Tell me, what are the first three things you would do to improve the operation of the company or to make it grow faster and better?'' The truth is that in almost every case you will find that once the employees have warmed up to you a little bit and become used to the fact that you are the new owner, they will suggest that the real roadblock to the successful growth of that company was the previous owner. It is almost always true. They will begin to tell you what the owner did wrong. It may not be wrong, but listen because if you want to keep your employees you have to do more than simply pay them well.

Remember, cash bonuses are better than salary increases and salary increases are better than equity participation. So be prepared to give cash bonuses frequently for good performance, particularly in the early weeks and months of your ownership. Nothing can seal the relationship faster than your recognition of good, solid performance when you see it. Also be aware that good employees are not only in it for the money. They need and want recognition and greater challenge. Most entrepreneurs never learn how to successfully share power or delegate authority. You can make a considerable positive impact through your ownership of this new business by recognizing the need that employees have for recognition and challenge and by delegating authority to them so that they can actually perform in their jobs. This will help them feel some sense of satisfaction above and beyond just taking home a paycheck.

Never buy with equity what you can buy with salary, and never buy with salary what you can buy with bonuses. (Cash bonuses are reported at the end of the year as Form 1099 income, not as ordinary wages and salaries.) By taking the bonus approach, the employee gets the immediate benefit of the entire cash amount rather than having withholding deducted before he gets it in his hand. Moreover, by giving cash, you can link immediately the performance and the receipt of a bonus in the mind of the employee. Do something good, get a bonus. Mess up, do not get a bonus.

It becomes very clear in their minds. It does not get attached to any particular date. It is not an annual review. It is not something that happens every Fourth of July or Easter or Halloween. It only happens when performance is there. Psychologically and practically, this kind of approach is far more effective and will have a far greater increase in productivity than giving everyone a 5 percent raise or making them part of a stock option program. Be sure to give the bonuses randomly enough so that they do not become predictable, or the strategy will lose its impact.

The Exit Plan

Taking a longer-range perspective, once you are in the business, you should start right from the beginning to develop an exit plan. Basically, your exit plan should coincide with the repayment of the debt. If you have encumbered the company with five-year debt, then your exit plan should be ready for execution in five years. This doesn't mean you have to sell a thriving business, only that you should be ready, willing and able to sell it. Let's take a look at that five-year period to see what you are actually trying to accomplish. You will find yourself saying a lot of interesting, bold, innovative and even creative things in your business plan about your three strategic goals and how you are going to meet them. But now you are actually there in the saddle. The responsibilities and decisions are yours.

What are you going to do? During the first year you are simply going to operate the business as it has been operated all along so that you can get to know it. Remember what Will Rogers said: "If it ain't broke, don't fix it." If you do not know for sure that something is wrong (and it may easily take you six months to a year to find out that something is wrong), do not get ambitious and try to improve the business. You bought it because it was a good, successful business. Let it go on being a good, successful business with you as the new owner.

During that first year become familiar with the feel of

it. How much cash comes in every day? What is the employee turnover like? What difficulties do you have in hiring, training and retraining? What kinds of problems do you encounter in getting customers and keeping customers? Are there any operations or production problems that need attention?

During the second and third years, you should reassess your three strategic goals from your business plan to make sure that they really are your top three priorities. You need to be sure that they should remain as the objectives for the business during the rest of your ownership. This is the period when you begin to prepare action implementation programs. This is when you develop the tactics to actually make the changes necessary to realize those strategic goals. In the fourth and fifth years, you should concentrate on the implementation and refinement of those tactical steps as you actually move toward your strategic goals. When all of the debt is paid off at the end of five years, you should be the owner of the business on a free-and-clear basis and in a position to sell it. The chances are high that you will have exhausted your bag of tricks. You do not want to stay at the party too long. Do not become like the entrepreneur who sold you his business.

Come into the business with a clear plan, execute your plan and get out.

You have a good, solid asset. Buy another one. Buy a bigger one, or relax, take some time off and do some fishing. Whatever you do, have a clear exit plan and stick to it. Certainly the lender is going to require that you have an exit plan. You should be prepared to sell the business at the end of the five-year period. You may have a little problem with the seller in the beginning. He may want to hang around and help out. You may have developed a wonderful working relationship. If so, you will be very fortunate. If your neat and orderly transition turns out to be not so neat or very orderly, what are you going to do about the seller? Many sellers want you to continue using their name on the building and on the business. They insist on it. It is called an immortality clause. They want to continue coming into the office. As long as they do and it is not clear who is the new boss, you are never going to be firmly in the saddle. If this happens, you have a very delicate situation to deal with because you need the seller as a source of information. He will not have had documented systems and procedures, so it will be necessary for you to create them as you go along. He will be the primary source of information for those systems and procedures that you are beginning to write down. As you begin to turn this into a professionally run business make sure that you do not turn a profitable mess into a well-organized, efficient failure.

In addition to consulting with the seller, you may want to deal with experts as outside consultants. This may be an ideal opportunity for you to begin to ease the seller out of the picture, especially if he has insisted on office space on the premises while you are there. Begin to set up meetings for him with consultants who are going to help you with various aspects of the business. Try Anchorage, Alaska, or Buenos Aires, Argentina. Schedule meetings at midnight or 4:00 A.M. I'm exaggerating a bit, but if the seller seems to be hanging on, do anything you can that is going to put a nice but firm burden on him so he gets the idea that he should ease out of the picture. But do it gently, so that you have him available as a source of information. You want to get the necessary information from him offsite in a nonintrusive, noninterruptive way. You need him, but you do not want him there looking over your shoulder, second-guessing you or giving your employees an alternative source of authority. Every time you try to implement a change, they can go to him to check it out. Then you bog down the progress of the business. In this case, the value of the business you have bought will diminish.

Most top executives, owners and entrepreneurs really earn their keep by making five or six key policy decisions each year. That is what you are there to do—make those decisions. You do not have to make all of the decisions right each and every year. Even the winningest football coaches in history, the Knute Rocknes or the Tom Landrys, do not win 100 percent of their games. You can get to be known as a really good coach if you win 50 percent to 60 percent of your games. And you can be a very successful entrepreneur if you can be right in half of your decisions. If you make 51 percent of your decisions correctly, you will be far ahead of the game. In a smaller business, making a decision is more important than procrastinating. Very little is gained by postponing a decision, but a lot of times small gears can come to an abrupt halt in the company if a decision is not made. So do not be afraid to make the decisions, even if you make the wrong ones. The chances are that you will have an opportunity to go back and correct the wrong ones you make before things go seriously awry. That is why, as you develop your business plan, you put in monitoring devices and reporting systems and share that information with your lender or your equity partners if you have them.

Monthly reports are a must. You can usually judge good entrepreneurs by how much they know about their daily cash flow. They almost always have an accurate picture whether they are in the office or on the road. They have a good sense of where everything is in their business. You should develop some of those habits yourself, because they are the ones that help you survive. Once a month you must review your budgeted expenses versus actual expenses and sales goals versus actual sales. These are your top and bottom lines. They are going to let you know if you are still on track. Once a quarter you must see a balance statement and a P & L. You will want to go over these with your CPA and your lender to make sure that you are still on track. But the most important thing of all is, you must have a commitment to a plan of action that forces you to get back on track if you begin to drift off. If sales are down by 5 percent or 10 percent from their targeted level, what do you do to get them back where they should be? Has the market changed? Is is necessary to revise the goals? If so, what impact is that going to have on the company? The solution might be to hire more salespeople or lay off production workers. But you must take decisive action.

If you encounter problems that are above and beyond your expertise, consult experts. Call in top-notch consultants in the area. Be sure that you check their references, experience and credentials. Make sure that what they have to offer is what you really need. Bring them in and listen carefully to what they have to say. If you have a particularly tough, thorny problem, it may be a good idea to bring in two or three on a short-term basis to get a second or third opinion on what you should be doing. Do not make the mistake that so many entrepreneurs make of trying to be your own brain surgeon. It is not really worth the money that you might save. By being well prepared, by asking cogent, organized, well-planned and thought-out questions of a consultant, you can probably get to the bottom of most of the problems you might encounter in your business in no more than a couple of hours. There are not that many different kinds of problems. A really talented, experienced consultant will be able to help you put your problem in perspective and get to the bottom of it. You may find that you do not want to implement any of the recommendations, but at least you should know what the problems are.

Remember that a good business is like a good milking stool. It rests on three legs. The first and most important of those legs is sales and marketing, because without customers you do not have a business. Next come operations and production, because if you do not produce goods or a service for your customers, you will not have a business for long. Finally comes finance and general administration, because you must know what you are doing, where you are going and whether or not you are making a profit. You will bring one set of skills, whether in sales/marketing, operations/production or finance/administration, to the business you buy. Do not ignore the other two legs of the stool or it will not support you. If you are strong in sales and marketing, make sure that you have adequate management and backup in the operations/production and finance/administration areas. This is particularly true for sales- and marketing-oriented people who do not like to listen to the bookkeeper. From this point of view, every sale results in 100 percent profit. It is not true. Operationally oriented owners frequently believe that if they simply build a better mousetrap, the world is going to beat a path to their door. They believe the products sell themselves, that they fall off the shelves into people's hands, that you do not really have to sell them. Why should you pay sales reps a horrendously large commission? This is not true. And finance/administrationally oriented owners frequently believe that their money is to be made on how they buy. They worship at the altar of cost control. This perception is not true. You have to control costs, but the key issue is how effective you are in reaching prospects, converting them into steady paying customers and keeping them that determines whether or not you have a successful business.

As you go through your first year and move into the second, third, fourth and fifth years, never lose sight of the three areas. Be aware. Continually monitor your activity and progress to make sure that your good, successful business continues to be good and successful. Pay attention to the details and work diligently so that the business grows with you. The value of the business asset you have purchased as your investment should increase as you move toward the point where you sell the business.

I have come to the end for now, but for you it is really just the beginning, because you are now going to go out into the real world and apply this material to buying your own first LBO. I want you to know, as you go through the steps that will lead you into the ownership of a successful business using little or none of your own money, that you must focus your effort and discipline, your will to succeed.

Never lose sight of your goal. And never give up hope. If you get stuck at any point, ask for help. Ask anyone who is available and has the experience in the area where you are stuck. Overcoming the fear and the "paralysis of analysis" does not require business expertise. What is important is your attitude and determination. I want you to start now to acquire your first LBO. I want you to make the commitment to do it. I want you to make the commitment to do it right, step by step through the entire process. I want you to persevere. I want you to have the persistence to see this through from its beginning until its end, until you end up as the owner of a successful business that you have acquired for little or none of your own money.

I have tried to give you all of the tools and information that I have found valuable in doing these deals. But I can't think of everything. New techniques are developed all the time, and each situation is unique. So if you get stuck at some point along the way or you want some more information on some aspect of doing your deal, write to me. I'll try to get back to you as soon as my schedule permits.

Good luck. And good hunting.

LIONEL HAINES
The Enterprise Network
710 Silver Spur Road, Suite 290
Rolling Hills Estates, CA 90274

■Appendix

Due Diligence Checklist

It is not necessary to answer each and every question for each and every business you examine. In fact, many of the questions may not apply to some of the businesses you will see. But you should at least review all of the questions each time you do your due diligence. And you should seek professional help from a competent attorney and CPA to help you with the complex technical, legal and accounting issues. But do not let them make your decisions for you. They are there to assist you, not run your life. Try to answer as many questions as you can. The point of this exercise is to make you comfortable with the business before you commit to buy it. In most cases, the owner will be the source for the answers. But you should also contact customers, suppliers and competitors, as well as trade associations and publications. Be careful not to put the deal in jeopardy by revealing your interest in buying the specific business you are currently examining.

General
1. What products or services are sold? List sales volume in dollars and by percent increase or decrease for each product or service for each of the last three years. Has the sales trend over the last three years been up (a positive sign), flat or down (a negative sign)? If selling into a single local market, is the trend in the local economy over the last three years up (a positive sign), flat or down (a very negative sign)?

2. In what way are products/services legally protected (patent, copyright, trademark, services mark) from competition? In what other ways are they proprietary? What makes the company unique or distinctive?

3. How is the business (both company and industry) affected by changes in the business cycle? Is it affected by seasonal changes?

4. What have been the major factors affecting the growth or decline of sales over the past five years?

5. How will the next five years of sales be different? Why? How will this forecast be reached?

6. Will any changes be required to reach forecast goals over the next five years? Why haven't these changes been made already?

7. What are the principal growth opportunities for new products/services or markets facing the company?

8. Are there any obvious or major gaps in the current products/services line?

9. Is the company or the industry less than seven years old? (A new company or industry is a very negative sign.)

10. When was the company founded? When was it incorporated? Where was it incorporated?

11. How many divisions, subsidiaries or secondary locations are there? Where are they located (specific, legal addresses)?

12. How was the company founded? What was its principal business purpose? Who were the founders and their successors? What has been the historical development of sales, profits and product/service lines?

13. Who are the shareholders? How much stock does each of them own? How many classes of stock are there? What is the total number of shares authorized in the treasury and outstanding for each class of stock?

14. Who are the officers and directors of the company? What are their addresses, phone numbers, positions and duties? Do they have a written profit-sharing plan (a negative sign)? Are key officers and directors secured with employment contracts (a very negative sign)? Are any key management positions occupied by members of the family or close personal friends of the owner (a very negative sign)?

15. Are there any other significant investments made by or affecting the company? Any special or unusual situations or circumstances?

16. What are the names, addresses and phone numbers of the company bank, CPA or auditor, attorney and any other advisor or consultant?

17. Is there an organizational chart showing all key employees, principals and officers, as well as number of employees by department or other unit? Do nonmanagement jobs require a low skill level (a positive sign) or a high skill level (a negative sign)?

18. Is there a healthy local labor market that can continue to supply employees for both replacement and projected growth (a positive sign)?

19. Is there an operations manual or book of systems and procedures? Is it complete and up to date? Are all tasks, work rules and regulations clearly defined?

20. Is there a list or brief summary of all employment contracts?

21. Will key managers stay after a change in ownership? Are there strong secondary managers, supervisors and foremen? Are new managers required?

22. How is the owner compensated? How much does he get in salary, bonuses, loans, advances, draws, consulting fees, automobile, airplane, boat, RV or trailer, life insurance, medical insurance, disability insurance, other insurance, pension plan, taxes, rent, home office, home or car phone, home utilities and all other indirect benefits?

23. How are other key managers compensated? How much do they get in direct and indirect payments? Is there an incentive plan? How are management benefits limited to top and key people?

24. Are offices sufficient in size and in level of accommodation for the company?

25. Are outside consultants used? How are they compensated? Are any under contract?

26. Are any of the employees unionized? When do union contracts expire? What has been the history of labor relations? Are there any present problems? Are any expected? How is overall employee morale? Is this a nonunion company in a unionized industry (a negative sign)?

27. What are the current payroll procedures?

28. What are the current practices and procedures for hiring, firing, advancement and promotion? Do they conform to local, state and federal regulations?

29. How is employee productivity, compared with industry norms? How long is the work week? What is the average hourly wage rate? What are the rates or salary ranges for each job classification?

30. What are the standard employee benefits? Are there any optional or alternative benefits? Are there any traditional parties, banquets, picnics, softball teams, etc.?

Marketing

1. Are there exclusive production or distribution rights to any products or services not available to any competition? Any private brands?

2. What market niches are served? Are advertising and promotional efforts aimed at these niches?

3. Are there competitors aiming at the same niches? Do they make the same claims about their products/services in ads and sales literature?

4. Are sales made directly by in-house sales force or through manufacturers' sales reps, jobbers or distributors? Are they made by bid? By telephone solicitation, mail order or through ads? Are other techniques used?

5. Are there any export opportunities in foreign markets? How about selling to the government?

6. Is the product/service sold because it is "better," "cheaper" or "faster"? Is it popular?

7. Is there a marketing plan with coordinated, measurable objectives? Does it cover all aspects of the marketing effort? Is there an implementation plan? Is it realistic?

8. Are there reliable sales forecasts used as a basis for planning and budgeting? Are they kept current?

9. Is effective, low-cost market research used to obtain quick input from customers?

10. Does the marketing program encourage repeat purchases and build loyalty?

11. Have any studies been done to determine the attitudes, beliefs and opinions of customers regarding product/service or company performance?

12. Are products/services properly positioned in the marketplace? Are any changes in product/service strategies necessary?

13. Are market niches divided into segments by product or service line on the basis of profitability? Does each niche or segment have its own strategy?

14. Have the life-cycle stages (introduction, growth, maturity, decline) been identified for each product/service? Have the appropriate marketing adjustments been made to reflect the different demands of the various stages?

15. Have marketing programs been developed to manage the level of demand and keep it in line with inventory, production or supply capabilities?

16. Has a legal audit of the marketing program been conducted to determine if all documents, claims, expressed or implied warranties and guarantees, local, state and federal regulations and voluntary industry standards have been met or are in full compliance?

17. Has each niche, segment or product line marketing program (strategy and activities) been adapted to meet the different or unique characteristics of each market served (government agencies, export, OEM, etc.)?

18. Has each product/service in the line been reviewed to determine specific sales performance and profitability? Have recommendations been made regarding the continuation, elimination or special promotion of each?

19. Is there a systematic program to generate new product ideas based on the expressed needs and wants of customers?

20. Are some aspects of the marketing operation (by niche or segment, by geography, by product/service, by distribution channel) more successful than others? Why?

21. Do salespeople require unique background, talents or abilities? Do they require lengthy, expensive training?

22. When and how are salespersons paid? What types of incentive programs are there?

23. Are sales and marketing personnel making the best use of their time on the job?

24. Is the best use being made of the telephone in marketing and sales?

25. Can existing sales expense levels be increased or decreased? What would be the impact on sales volume and profit margins?

26. What is the policy on warranties, guarantees, service and returns?

27. How are new products developed?

28. If retail, should more stores be opened? Should existing stores be closed? Is there a franchise potential? For each store, what is the size and demographics of the trade area?

Advertising & Promotion

1. Is there a regular, budgeted advertising program?

2. Is there an advertising agency? (Get name, address, contact person's name and media list.) Is the agency doing a good job? Is the program ready for a new theme?

3. What is the total dollar amount of the advertising and sales promotion budget? What is the budget as a percentage of sales? How does the budget break down (in percentages) for various activities—i.e., ads (newspaper, magazine, radio, TV, telephone and trade directories), direct marketing (mail, telephone), trade shows, premiums, special promotions, co-op ad programs, brochures and price lists?

4. Is co-op advertising available from suppliers? In what form and under what conditions?

5. Is the current advertising program on target in terms of sales impact and budget? Is there an evaluation mechanism set up to measure results? Could it be made more effective for the same or less money?

6. What is the image projected by the logo, letterhead, brochures, catalogs, price lists and other printed materials? Is it right for the market? Should it be changed?

7. How are sales leads generated? How are new accounts developed? Who does the development and what does it cost (total dollars per account)? Are prospects and existing accounts being followed up regularly in a coordinated or comprehensive way?

8. Are testimonials used? How are they obtained? What do they cost? Are they effective?

9. Is there a regular, steady public relations program? Are new product/service press releases sent out regularly?

10. How many trade shows are attended? Are there others that should be added? Any to be dropped? How effective are they?

11. Is direct mail a significant marketing tool? Which mailing lists are being used? Where did the names come from? Are mailings being made at the lowest cost? What have the response rates been? How do they compare with industry norms?

12. Is the company's reputation in the industry good or bad? (Bad is very negative, good is neutral.)

13. Are special promotions used? Are they effective? Should they be increased?

Customers

1. What types of businesses or kinds of people buy the products/services?

2. How do customers use the products/services?

3. What percentage of total sales volume does each type or kind of customer buy?

4. What are the buying motives of the customers (price, quality, service, distribution, delivery, terms, sale source, etc.)?

5. Who are the major customers? What percentage of total sales have each of the ten largest customers accounted for over the last three years? Does any customer account for 10 percent or more of total sales (a very negative sign)?

6. Would any of the major customers stop buying if the company was sold?

7. Are any of the major customers related to any of the present owners in any way? What impact would a sale of the business have on them?

8. How many active customer accounts are there?

9. How often do customers reorder?

10. What is the average dollar value of an initial sale? Of a typical reorder?

11. What percentage of total sales are initial orders and what percentage repeat sales?

12. What is being done to encourage repeat sales? (It is a positive sign if 50 percent or more place repeat orders.)

13. Are there written sales contracts with any accounts? For how long? For how much? When do contracts expire? What

are the renewal conditions or options? Are there unwritten verbal agreements?

14. How much of the total sales effort does the owner handle personally (10 percent or more is a very negative sign)?

15. What kind of effort and what people will be needed to replace present ownership in sales and customer relations?

16. Are prospective customers easy to identify (a positive sign)?

17. Do 5 percent or more of the customers require special credit terms, discounts or special billing procedures (a negative sign)?

18. How is knowledge of customer buying patterns used to speed acceptance of new products/services or other innovations and changes?

19. Are customers loyal or is there a big turnover?

20. What is customer attitude toward the company? How could it be improved?

21. How can sales to existing customers be increased?

22. How can the average order be increased?

23. What percentage of total accounts are new customers each year for the past three years?

Pricing

1. What is the price and profit margin for every product or service in the line? Are there different price lists for different market segments?

2. What has been the annual increase or decrease (in percentages) in prices for each of the past three years?

3. In the industry, are prices generally stable or volatile?

4. How would a price increase affect sales volume?

5. At what annual rate (in percentages) do you expect prices to change over the next five years? Why?

6. Should prices be increased or decreased on any products or services?

7. Are there fair trade laws that affect prices?

8. Are there bidding procedures or conditions that affect prices?

9. Is pricing determined by large national compromise (a negative sign)?

10. Is pricing opportunistic (as high as the market will bear) and controlled by a few highly skilled or well-connected salespersons (a negative sign)?

11. Are products/services priced in accordance with their value in the market (a positive sign)?

12. Are products/services priced for the top of the market (a positive sign) or the middle of the market (neutral) or the bottom of the market (a negative sign)?

13. Can comparison buyers easily shop competitors for price, benefits and features (a negative sign)?

Distribution
1. What are the specific geographic selling areas covered?

2. What are the present methods of distribution (direct sales, dealerships, wholesalers or jobbers, in-house sales force or independent reps)? If more than one method is being used, compare number of sales, percentage of sales dollars and percentage of profits from each method. Are other methods effective?

3. Are all markets being covered? Are there export or import opportunities? Should a distribution change be considered? Should any market be eliminated? How can methods of obtaining distributors or dealers be improved?

Competitors

1. Who are the competitors, both the industry leaders and similar-sized firms? Where are they located? Can anyone there be contacted?

2. List all competitors by estimated sales, profits and market shares (in percentages).

3. How are the competitors' products or services promoted, packaged, priced or distributed differently? Are major competitors selling service (a positive sign) or price (a negative sign)?

4. Obtain competitors' catalogs, brochures and price lists. Compare strategies, positioning, appeal and value (price, packaging, product utility).

5. What is the competitive structure of the industry? Is it highly concentrated and dominated by a few companies? Are these companies major national or international companies? Is the industry fragmented with many similar-sized firms serving niche markets? What kind of industry cooperation exists?

6. Are major competitors in an expansion phase? Are they actively increasing their market share?

Physical Facilities

1. Where are the principal business premises (street address, city, state, ZIP)?

2. What is the zoning?

3. Is it owned or leased? If owned, get legal description, exact form of ownership and name of owner.

4. Get the amount, terms and conditions of any mortgages, especially those relating to payoff of balances and changes of ownership.

5. Is there a recent appraisal? For what purpose was it made? What do comparable properties cost?

6. What are the property taxes? How are they collected and paid?

7. If leased, get a copy or full description of the terms and conditions of the lease, especially increases in rent. Does the lease require a personal guarantee? Does the lease require that the building be restored to its original condition? Are parking spaces guaranteed? Does the tenant have the right to remove furniture and fixtures or must they remain at the end? What happens if the building is partially or totally destroyed or condemned? How about sublease?

8. Are there any other facilities or secondary premises? How are they owned or leased?

9. Is there a set of plans and drawings?

10. How many square feet in the building? How many square feet of land? How much office space and warehouse space in the building? How many loading and shipping docks?

11. What is the condition of the premises? What improvements have been made? Are any repairs required? How are janitorial and housekeeping functions handled?

12. What kinds and amounts of insurance coverage are there? Who are the carriers? Who is the agent? What are the costs, terms and conditions of each policy? Is the coverage adequate?

13. Are the fire protection and safety devices adequate? Do the sprinklers work? Have fire extinguishers been put where required? Are they regularly recharged? Is there an alarm sys-

tem? Are smoke detectors used? How is local police and fire protection?

14. Are the electrical, water, sewer and gas utilities and hookups adequate for present use? For future growth? Are they in full compliance with all local, state and federal laws, rules and regulations? If not, how important is full compliance? What will it cost?

15. What percentage of the current premises are being used? What is the potential capacity of the facilities at full use? For how long will the current premises be adequate? Is there room for expansion at the present location? Where would the company relocate if it became necessary? How much would it cost to relocate? What impact would it have on business operations and cash flow?

16. Where are the nearest available public warehouse or storage facilities? Is the location served by rail, freight common carrier, parcel delivery services, boat or barge transport, air freight, etc.? Is the local post office near? How are freight delivery rates compared to those of other locations and competitors?

17. Is this the best location to reach the market or markets served by the company? If retail, check vehicle and pedestrian traffic flow. Is there enough parking? Is it free or paid? Is the store visibility and signage as good as it can be? Is the area new, mature or declining? What will it be like in five or ten years? How is public transportation access? Where are competitors located?

18. Are all raw materials or merchandise necessary for operations readily available at this location? Will this continue to be true? What about expansion?

19. Is there a sufficient quantity of trained employees available in the local labor pool? How do prevailing salaries and wage rates compare with other locales? With competitors?

20. Are local housing, schools, shopping, cultural and community activities adequate for employees? Is this considered to be a desirable location to work in?

Legal

1. In which state or states is the business incorporated? In which states is it registered or otherwise qualified to do business? What must be done to continue operations?

2. Does the company comply with all local laws and regulations? Are all necessary permits in order (zoning, land use, business use, business license, elevators, special equipment, etc.)? What kind of negotiations are required to obtain these permits? What inspections? How often?

3. Does the company comply with state and federal laws, regulations and requirements (consumer protection, fair trade, pollution control, duties, tariffs and quotas or other regulatory agencies)? How often must compliance be demonstrated? How much does it cost?

4. What are the terms and conditions of all the existing contracts with customers, suppliers, subcontractors, distributors, agents, reps, advertising agencies and media? Are there any government contracts? Are there any contingent or implied contracts or oral agreements? What impact will a change of ownership have on them?

5. Are all employee benefit plans fully documented and funded (insurance, pension, retirement, profit sharing, bonus, stock options or warrants, ESOP)?

6. Do all employees have required licenses, credentials, permits and registrations? Are they current?

7. Is there a union contract? What about "right to work" laws?

8. What are the current regulations concerning employee minimum wage, maximum work hours, overtime, etc.?

9. Are there OSHA or other health, safety and working conditions, laws, rules and regulations to be met? Is the company in compliance? If not, how much will it cost to comply?

10. Are there any discrimination (age, race, sex) or child labor issues involved here?

11. Is there a complete list of all patents (by number) and patents pending, copyrights, trade and service marks, franchise agreements, trade secrets or license agreements? Are they legal and current? Can they be transferred in their present form? At what cost?

12. Are there any pending pieces of legislation, changes in government regulations or in the business environment, that may impact this company?

Operations & Production

1. Who are the major vendors and sources of supply? What is the nature of the present relationship with them? Would the relationship continue on the same basis if the business was sold?

2. Are there second sources of backup suppliers for the goods, services and raw materials necessary to run the business? Are there any sole source suppliers (a negative sign)? Are suppliers abundant and competitive (a positive sign)?

3. Are any of the suppliers members of the owner's family or close friends? Can they be easily replaced as suppliers?

4. What is the nature of supplier trade practices? Do key suppliers have very high minimum order requirements or unreasonable credit terms? Do suppliers cooperate in terms of advertising, service, warranties, etc.? Will vendors supply materials or goods on consignment or floor plan basis?

5. For each product or service offered, list the labor cost, materials cost and production overhead cost for each of the last three years in dollars and as a percentage of gross sales.

6. What are the prospects for labor, material and overhead costs for the next five years? In what areas could reductions or economies be made? Would they require any initial investment?

7. Are production schedules set up and followed?

8. How many shifts currently work? What is the maximum capacity at this level? How many shifts could be added? What would the capacity be at this level? Does the flexibility exist to increase or decrease production while maintaining profit margins? What is the break-even point at minimum production?

9. What percentage of the finished product is purchased as subassemblies and finished components? How much is actually manufactured in-house?

10. Could operations be made more efficient? At what cost?

11. Are materials handled and stored efficiently and safely? How is scrap and waste handled?

12. Are preventive maintenance and safety procedures followed regularly? How much time is lost due to downtime or work injury?

13. What production equipment (owned and leased) is there at present? (List each piece by type, manufacturer, condition, age, date purchased, price and stock number. Also list all tooling, jigs, dies and related fixtures.) What is the production capacity of this existing equipment?

14. What are the roadblocks to maximum efficient production? Is there an ongoing program to improve productivity, systems and procedures?

15. What is the average time it takes to fill an order? What are normal lead times for each aspect or phase of operations? How can they be improved? Are there time/motion studies?

16. Is an inventory kept? How often is a physical count inventory taken? How is inventory controlled? How many times a year does inventory turn over?

17. What type of cost or other controls exist?

18. Is there a good system to coordinate production and sales?

19. How much is spent on research and development in dollars and as a percentage of sales?

20. How many people work in R & D? What is the relationship between skilled and unskilled workers here?

21. Is there a new invention or discovery agreement with employees?

22. Is there any technology licensing arrangement?

23. Is the current R & D budget sufficient to maintain the company's competitive position in the market?

Financial
1. Does the company have current financial statements (balance sheet, income statement, statement of changes in financial position)? Get complete financial statements for the past three years, including pretax net profits in actual dollars and as a percentage of sales. Get projections on an annual basis of sales, profits and cash flow for the next five years.

2. Is the rescheduled pretax net profit for the most recent year less than 5 percent (a very negative sign) or more than 10 percent (a positive sign)?

3. Has the profit trend been up (a positive sign), down (a very negative sign) or flat for the past three years?

4. What has been the company's policy regarding dividend payment for the past three years? Has this policy been carried out? Why not?

5. Is the cash flow positive nine months or more each year (a positive sign)? Is the cash flow negative six months or more of each year (a very negative sign)?

6. What is the minimum sales volume necessary to break even? Are fixed costs more than 60 percent of total costs (a negative sign)?

7. Have the financial statements been audited or prepared by an independent CPA? If so, do the footnotes state any qualifications, exceptions, disclaimers or other unusual matters?

8. Are there any significant changes (plus or minus 10 percent) in sales, expenses or profits in the last three years? Why? Check for each category, also by quarter, by geographic area, by major customers, and by product or product line.

9. Have there been any sales to affiliated or associated persons, friends, family members or entities controlled by them, or to competitors? Has there been any other unusual sales activity? Why?

10. Is there a warranty or guarantee program? Is the reserve fund adequately funded? What has been the payout experience? How does the program compare with that of others in the industry? Should it be modified in any way?

11. Is there an order backlog? How does it break down by product or product line? What provisions exist for price increases if costs increase? What about decrease in cost or price? Does the company produce primarily against orders or for inventory?

12. Has the owner reduced any fixed or variable expenses of a discretionary nature that could have an impact on future profits (for example, advertising cost by 50 percent)?

13. Has the owner used sales or profit forecasts in the past? How have the actual results compared with his forecasts? Why?

14. Have there been any extraordinary charges or credits, catch-up adjustments, prior-period adjustments or other nonrecurring or unusual items during the past three years? Why?

15. Do foreign customers play a role in company sales? Are orders denominated in U.S. or foreign currencies? Has anything been done to hedge the risks of exchange rate fluctuation?

16. Have any "miscellaneous" income or expense items exceeding 3 percent of total income or expenses been recorded in the last three years? Why?

17. Is there a contingency plan for the reduction of overhead and other expenses in the event of a general recession, an industry downturn or a loss of a major market segment? What severance payments are required by employment contracts or union agreements in the event of layoffs?

18. Are 75 percent or more of the retained earnings reinvested in plant, machinery, equipment or improvement (a very negative sign)?

19. Do fixed assets account for 60 percent or more of the total (a negative sign)? Do current assets account for 50 percent or more of the total (a positive sign)? Do other assets account for 10 percent or more total assets (a very negative sign)?

20. Do any of the company's banks require compensating balances or have withdrawal restrictions? Are these provisions adequate and reliable?

21. What are the accounts receivable by customer, by product or product line and by geographic area? Have there been any significant changes over the last three years? Why?

22. Is the reserve for doubtful accounts less than 3 percent (a positive sign) or more than 10 percent (a negative sign)? Review bad-debt list for last three years.

23. What are the normal credit policies and terms? Have there been any changes in the past three years? Why? Are there any "special" terms in effect? Who sets them? Why?

24. Have there been any accounts receivable factored, pledged, sold, hypothecated or borrowed against with or without recourse in the past three years? If so, review details. Is there any current contingent liability from these activities?

25. Are there any exceptionally large or long overdue balances in the accounts receivable? Why? What has been done or is being done to collect?

26. Does the company hold any collateral against debts? What is the basis for determining its market value? When was this last done?

27. Are there any "miscellaneous" receivables due from the owner, other officers or directors, shareholders, employees, subsidiary or affiliated entities, etc.? What provisions exist for their payment? Is documentation complete and up to date?

28. Is there an inventory analysis by product or product line or other relevant categories for each of the last three years? Have turnover ratios been calculated? Is there an inventory aging analysis? What about obsolete, slow-moving, bill-and-hold and expired-sale-contract inventories on hand? Should any of this be written off? What are current policies and procedures?

29. How much inventory has been written off each year for the last three years? Have there been any inventory adjustments or reserves transactions in the last three years (book vs. actual, price errors, under- or over-absorbed costs, changes in accounting policies or practices)?

30. Is there a cost system? Is it a standard cost system? If so, how often is it updated? What are the procedures for gathering and evaluating standard cost data? Is batch costing used

as a reliability check? How often? What variances exist? How are they accounted for?

31. Are there perpetual inventory records? In what form? Are they used for interim financial statements?

32. Are there any outstanding contracts or commitments for the large-scale or bulk purchase or sale of inventory items?

33. Has any inventory been pledged or otherwise offered as security for debt or line of credit financing in the last three years? If so, review details.

34. Is there any inventory held on consignment or consigned to others at present? In the past? If so, review details.

35. Are there or have there been any significant long-term contracts? How are they accounted for, on completion or percentage of completion? Are there adequate provisions for losses or uncompleted contracts? What has been the company's actual profit or loss experience with long-term contracts over the past three years?

36. Have there been any major purchases or sales of fixed assets or real estate in the last three years?

37. At what book values are fixed assets and real estate currently carried by item? Is any asset not carried at cost?

38. Have all obsolete plant and equipment been written off? Has depreciation been accelerated where technology changes will require early replacement?

39. Are fixed assets or real estate underutilized? Why?

40. What portion of the operations are manual, semiautomated and fully automated? How much would it cost to fully automate? Could that investment be returned in less than eighteen months?

41. Are the estimated useful lives of assets currently used for book depreciation reasonable? Are any major assets due for replacement or other significant expense in the next five years?

42. How do recent appraisals and tax assessment valuations relate to original costs and current market values of major assets? Watch especially for recent purchases.

43. How are property items capitalized?

44. Have any fixed assets or real estate been pledged or otherwise used as security for debt or lines of credit? If so, review details.

45. Are there any prepaid expenses, deferred charges or other assets (analyze by major category such as insurance, taxes, interest, etc.) currently on the books?

46. Is there adequate insurance coverage? Do policy amounts relate to realistic replacement costs or market values? Get a complete list of policies, terms, conditions, costs and agents. Review for completeness and adequacy.

47. Is there a list of accounts payable by supplier and by age? If not, can one be prepared?

48. Are there any special credit terms with existing suppliers? What are they? How long will they last? How did they come about?

49. Is there a policy regarding prompt payment for cash discounts? List all cash discounts lost or taken over the past three years.

50. Are there accrued liabilities other than taxes? Review advertising, insurance, payroll and interest categories especially. Are there any others?

51. Have appropriate accruals been made for pensions, retroactive wage adjustments, co-op ad programs, pending litigation, guarantees and warranties, sales allowances and credits, environmental or waste contamination, or foreign currency losses?

52. Are there any significant contingent liabilities pending? If so, review details.

53. Are federal and state income tax statements available for the last three years? If so, review for unusual items.

54. Is there a list of all federal and state taxes due by category, due date, amount due, amount accrued and any prior-period delinquencies? If not, prepare such a list.

55. Is there a summary of all long- and short-term debt by holder, showing terms and conditions, maturities, current balances due and effective interest rates? Review all loan agreements for convertibility, collateral, default procedures and any restrictions on company activity such as compensating balances, working capital requirements, permitted debt or dividend limits, assumability or due on sale provisions, prepayment premiums, sinking fund requirements.

56. Are all covenants of all loans and financing agreements currently being met? Are there any definitional inadequacies in the agreements that could cause problems?

57. Are there separate equity accounts? If so, review activity and transactions for the last three years.

58. Is there a disaster recovery plan? If computers are used, is there an off-site data storage program? Is it adequate and up to date? Is it used regularly?

59. Have there been any changes in accounting policies, practices or procedures that have had a significant impact on profits in the last three years? If so, review details.

60. Is there a list of nonrecurring adjustments for the most recent years? If so, review details.

61. Are there any generally accepted accounting practices followed by most firms in the industry that are not being followed by the company (for example, inventory valuation, additions to inventory for warehousing, handling, interest and other carrying costs, methods of depreciation, asset classification, investment valuation basis, R & D expenditures)?

62. Is the company using alternative accounting methods where preferable methods exist? Check especially inventory valuation, depreciation (methods and lives), depletion, pension cost provisions and realization of income in the sale of products, services or assets, sales to affiliates, long-term contracts, cash discounts and investment credits.

63. If the values of all the current and fixed assets are brought up to present fair market values (rescheduled), can they be sold or pledged for enough cash to make the down payment and still provide working capital for the business? If not, the terms are wrong or the price is too high.

64. Will the owner finance (carry back paper) at least 75 percent of the purchase price? If not, what does that say about the owner's confidence in the future of the business?

▪Index

ABCO, 114
Accounting policies, 200–201
Accounts payable, 52–53, 199
Accounts payable aging
    analysis, 52–53
    obtaining, 146
Accounts receivable, 47–48,
    196, 197
    factoring, 88–89
Accounts receivable aging
    analysis, 47
    obtaining, 146
Advertising: *see* Classified
    advertising
Advertising and promotion, 59
    questions in due diligence,
    183–84
Agreements: *see* Documents
    and agreements
Ambitions, personal, 24–25
American Appraisal, 50, 124
American Can Company, 7
Appraisers, 64, 124–25
Arbitration provision, 165
Archimedes (quoted), 3
Assets, 44, 46, 196, 198, 199,
    201
    accounts receivable, 47–48
    cash, 46–47

fixed, 49–52, 92–94
    hidden, 50–52
    inventory, 48–49
    net current, 73, 76–77
    net current value, 78
    net long-term, 73, 76–77
    schedule of, in financial
    package, 124–25
"Assets only," 153–55
Associations: *see* Trade
    associations
Attorneys, 40–41, 160–61,
    165–66
Audits:
    businessman's, 64
    tax, 44
Automobile expenses, 60

Balance sheet analysis, 42, 43,
    44–55
    assets, 44, 46–52
    checklist, 54–55
    current ratio, 54
    liabilities, 44–46, 52–54
    sample, 45
    summary of, 54
Balance sheet projection, 123
Balloon notes, 98–99

Bankers, 32
Banks, 115
Beer and wine wholesaler
businesses, 36
Biological products industry,
36
Bonds:
junk, 105
U.S. Treasury, 110
zero coupon, 98–99, 110
Brokerage fees, 165
Brokers:
business opportunity, 33
loan, 116
Business Rates & Data—Part I,
21, 37
Business Week, Inc., 23
Businesses:
buying established, 4–6
cycles, 178
evaluating, 69–83
middle market, 6–8
most likely to survive, 35–36
personal ambitions about, 24–
25
privately owned, 58–59
privately owned, most
successful, 36
pursuing, 25–38
selling, reasons for, 15–16
starting, 4–5
see also Businesses, owning
and running; Companies;
Industries
Businesses, owning and
running, 167–74
cash bonuses, 168–69
consultants, outside, 171,
173
employees, meeting with,
167–68
exit plan, 169–70
finance and administration,
173–74

monthly reports, 172–73
operations and production,
173–74
policy decisions, 171–72
sales and marketing, 173–74
seller, dealing with, 170–71
Buyer obligations, 164
Buyout Publications (address),
38

Calculating and accounting
machines industry, 36
Candidates, leveraged buyout,
6–17
divestitures of divisions, 7
example, 8–16
middle market businesses, 6–
8
privately held companies, 8
public companies, small, 7–8
Cap rates, 74, 79, 83
Capitalization, 79
Cash, 46–47, 88
bonuses, 168–69
Cash-creation techniques:
accounts receivable factoring,
88–89
cash, 88
fixed assets, 92–94
inventory, 90–92
notes receivable, 89–90
Cash-deferral techniques:
agreements with seller, 100–
103
debt, 95–97
earn-outs, 99–100
installment notes, 97–99
perks, 94–95
royalties, 99
Cash flow, 195
discounted, as evaluation
method, 74–75
projections, 75, 123

Certified public accountants,
40–41
source of leads, 32
Classified advertising:
local business ads, 32–33
responding to, 27–28
running, 26–27
Columbia Books, Inc. (address),
37
Companies:
divestitures of divisions,
7
history of, 178
privately held, 8
public, small, 7–8
see also Businesses;
Industries
Compensation, 148, 180
Competitors:
obtaining information about,
146–47
questions about in due
diligence, 188
Conduct of business pending
transfer, 164
Confidentiality agreement,
152–53
Conflicts of interest, 164
Consultants, 171, 173, 180
business, as lead source, 32
Consulting agreements, 102–103
Consumer Price Index, 72, 93
Contingency plans, 126
Corporations, forming new,
155–56
Customers:
dealing with in liquidation,
12–13
questions about in due
diligence, 185–86

Deal analysis: see Due diligence
Deal closing, 152–66

confidentiality agreement,
152–53
employee confidentiality
agreement, 160
letter of intent, 153–59
letter of nonproprietary
interest, 152–53
personnel policies and
procedures, 160
purchase and sale agreement,
160, 161–62, 163–65
sequence of events, 161–62
trust security agreement, 160
Deal structuring, 85–110
cash-creation techniques, 87–
94
cash-deferral techniques,
94–103
fraudulent conveyance, 85–87
sample, step-by-step, 105–10
Debts:
assume, 96
as cash-deferral tool, 95–97
collateral substitution, 96–97
miscellaneous and bad, 63
questions in due diligence, 200
refinance short-term to long-
term, 95–97
Depreciation, 60
Directories, 28–29
company, 37–38
intermediaries, 38
Directory of Intermediaries, 38
Distribution, 187–88
Documents and agreements:
confidentiality agreement,
152–53
consulting agreement, 102–
103
employee confidentiality
agreement, 160
employment agreement, 101–
102
letter of intent, 153–59

Documents and agreements (*cont'd*)
letter of nonproprietary interest, 152–53
not-to-compete agreement, 100–101, 165
personnel policies and procedures, 160
promissory notes, 163
purchase and sale agreement, 160, 161–62, 163–65
trust security agreement, 160
Drugstore businesses, 35
Due diligence, 39–68
appraisers to confirm assets, 64
businessman's audit, 64
final, 161
financial statements, 42–64
former employees, contacting, 67
main marketing issues, 64–65
operations issues, key, 66
organizational issues, key, 66–67
Uniform Commercial Code filings, 64
see also Due diligence checklist
Due diligence checklist, 177–201
advertising and promotion, 183–84
competitors, 188
customers, 185–86
distribution, 187–88
facilities, physical, 188–91
financial, 194–201
general, 177–80
legal, 191–92
marketing, 181–83
operations and production, 192–94
pricing, 186–87
Dun & Bradstreet, 28, 34, 35, 57
address, 38

Dun & Bradstreet/Small Business Administration, 36

Earnings and cash flow techniques, 74
Earn-outs, 99–100
Electrical measuring devices industry, 37
Electronic computing equipment industry, 36
Electronic connectors industry, 36
Electronics manufacturing and distributing businesses, 36
Employee confidentiality agreement, 160
Employees:
dealing with in liquidation, 11–12
former, contacting, 67
meeting with, as new owner, 167–68
questions about in due diligence, 180
Employment agreement, 101–102, 165
Employment contracts, 179
Encyclopedia of Associations, 37
Enterprise Network, 36
Equipment rental, 60
Equipment rental businesses, 36
Equity kicker, 128–32
calculating sample, 131–32
Evaluation methods, 70–83
comparable sales value, 71–72
discounted cash flow, 74–75
excess earnings, 75–82
income capitalization, 74
liquidation value, 70–71
net present value, 72–74
replacement cost, 71

Excess earnings method, 75–82
  calculating, 77–80
  example, step-by-step, 80–82
  price range, determining, 82
  summarization, 82–83

Facilities, physical, 188–91
Fees and services, 60–61
Finance and administration,
    173–74
Finance companies, 114, 115–16
Financial leverage, 3
Financial package, 123–28
  checklist, 128
  contingency plans in, 126
  history and background in,
    124
  key managers, biographies of
    in, 124
  market analysis in, 126–28
  pro forma financial statement
    in, 123
  strategy statement in, 124,
    125
Financial partners, 128–29
Financial publications, 23
Financial questions in due
    diligence, 194–201
  accounting policies, 200–201
  accounts payable, 199
  accounts receivable, 196, 197
  assets, 196, 198, 199, 201
  credit policies, 197, 199
  debt, 200
  income taxes, 200
  insurance, 199
  inventory, 197, 198
  liabilities, 199, 200
  operations, 198
  owner financing, 201
  profit, 194, 195
  sales, 195
  statements, 194, 195

Financial statements, 42–64, 195
  balance sheet analysis, 44–55
  income statement analysis,
    55–64
Financial structure, 147–48
Financing, 111–32
  equity kicker, 128–32
  plan package, 123–28
Fixed assets: see Assets
Forbes, 23
Form 1099, 168
Fortune, 23
Fraudulent conveyance, 85–87
Fringe benefits: see Perks
Fuel oil dealer businesses, 35
Funeral home businesses, 35
Furniture manufacturing
    businesses, 36

Gale Research company
    (address), 37
GE Credit, 114
Glass and concrete
    manufacturing businesses,
    36
Gross profit margin, 57

Heller International, 114
History and background, 124
Hotel businesses, 35, 36

Icahn, Carl, 3, 104
Immortality clause, 171
Income capitalization, 74
Income statement analysis, 42,
    43, 44, 55–64
  advertising, 59
  automobile expenses, 60
  debts, miscellaneous and bad,
    63
  depreciation, 60

Income statement analysis
  (cont'd)
  equipment rental, 60
  fees and services, 60–61
  gross profit margin, 57
  insurance, 61
  interest, 61
  net profits, 63–64
  other revenues, 57
  postage and freight, 62
  rent, 62
  repairs, 62
  salaries, 59
  sample, 56
  supplies, 62
  taxes, 62
  telephone, 62
  travel and entertainment, 62–
    63
  utilities, 62
Income statement projections,
    123
Income tax statements, 200
Indemnification and resolution
    of disputes, 164
Industries, 19–38
  age, 178
  analysis of, 21–23
  consolidated, 20–21
  fastest growth, 36–37
  fragmented, 21
  trends of, 20
  see also Businesses;
    Companies
Installment notes:
  annuity for security, 97
  as cash-deferral tool, 97–99
  senior or subordinated debt,
    97
Insurance, 61
  questions in due diligence,
    199
Insurance salesman, 32
Interest, 61

Internal Revenue Service:
  ruling 5960, 82
  Section 337, 154
Inventory, 48–49, 197, 198
  borrow against, 91–92
  on consignment basis, 91
  liquidate, 91
  sell back to supplier, 91
  seller keeping, 90–91

Junk bonds, 105

Labor market, 179
Landry, Tom, 172
Laundry and dry cleaner
    businesses, 35
LBO: see Leveraged buyouts
Lead sources, 31–32
Legal questions in due diligence,
    191–92
Lenders, 111–13
  finance companies, 114, 115–
    16
  finding, 116–20
  types, 113
  see also Lenders, secured
Lenders, secured:
  corporate-finance, 117–18
  expectations from you,
    121–28
  finding, 118–20
  "old-school," 117
Letter of commitment,
    conditional, 145
Letter of intent, 151, 153–59, 161
  "assets only," 153–55
  form new corporation, 155–56
  sample, 157–59
  tax-loss carry-forward deals,
    255
Letter of nonproprietary
    interest, 152–53

Letter writing, 28–30
  sample, 29–30
Leveraged buyouts, 3–4
  candidates, 6–17
  deal closing, 152–66
  deal structuring, 85–110
  due diligence, 39–68
  evaluating a business, 69–83
  financing, 111–32
  industry selection, 19–38
  negotiating process, 133–51
Liabilities, 44–46, 52–54, 199, 200
  accounts payable, 52–53
  accrued, 53
  footnotes, 53
  long-term, 53
  undisclosed, 164
  unrecorded, 53–54
Liquidation auction, 70–71
Liquidation process, 10–14
  customers, dealing with, 12–13
  employees, dealing with, 11–12
  perks, loss of, 13–14
  suppliers, dealing with, 13
Liquidation value, 70–71
Lithographic platemaking services industry, 37
Loan packagers, lenders through, 116
Loans, types of, 114–16

Management, key:
  biographies of, 124
  questions in due diligence, 179
Managerial structure, 147
Manufacturers Register, 38
Marketing:
  analysis, 126–28
  issues, 64–65

Marketing question in due diligence, 181–83
  export opportunities, 181
  new product development, 183
  production or distribution rights, 181
  programs, 182
  sales forecasts, 181
  sales personnel, 183
Medicinals and botanicals industry, 36
Meetings: see Negotiation process; Negotiation tips
Metal products manufacturing businesses, 36
Million Dollar Directory, Volumes 1, 2, and 3, 37–38
My Fair Lady, 134

National Commercial Finance Association, 118
National Trade and Professional Associations of the United States, 37
Negotiation process, 133–51
  accounts payable, 146
  accounts receivable, 146
  competition, 146–47
  establishing relationship and credibility, 138–40
  financial structure, 147–48
  letter of intent, 151
  managerial structure, 147
  meeting times, 134
  note taking, 144–45
  perks, presenting, 149
  plant tour, 143–44
  purchase price, final, 150–51
  qualifying seller, 140–43
Negotiation tips, 135–38
Net income figure, pretax, 75–76

Net present value, 72–74
Net profit, 63–64, 194
Net tangible worth, 73, 76
Net worth, 73
Newsletters, 21–23
  questions to ask, 22–23
  run classified ads in, 26–27
1985 U.S. Industrial Outlook, 37
Not-to-compete agreement, 100–101
  in purchase and sale agreement, 165
Note taking tips, 137, 144–45
Notes:
  balloon, 98–99
  payable, 52
  promissory, 163
  see also Installment notes; Notes receivable
Notes receivable, 47–48
  calling or selling, 89–90

Oil production businesses, 36
Operations and production, 173–74
  issues, 66
Operations and production questions in due diligence, 192–94
  research and development, 194
  schedules and equipment, 193–94
  supplier trade policies, 192
  supply sources, 192
Operations manual, 179
Optical instruments and lenses industry, 36
Organizational analysis, 147
Organizational chart, 179
Organizational issues, 66–67

Perks, 5–6
  as cash-deferral tool, 94–95
  losing in liquidation, 13–14
  presenting, 149
Personal service businesses, 36
Personnel policies and procedures, 160
Pharmaceuticals manufacturing businesses, 36
Pickens, T. Boone, 3, 104
Plant tours, 143–44
Postage and freight, 62
Price:
  final, 150–51
  range, determining, 82
Price/earnings ratio, 74
Pricing questions in due diligence, 186–87
Pro forma financial statement, 123
Products/services, 177, 178, 181, 182, 187
Profit and loss (P&L): *see* Income statement
Profit-sharing plan, 179
Promissory notes, 163
Publications:
  company directories, 37–38
  industrial, 37
  M & A intermediaries, 38
  trade, 37
  trade associations, 37
Purchase and sale agreement, 160, 161–62, 163–65
  arbitration provision, 165
  brokerage fees, 165
  conduct of business pending transfer, 164
  conflicts of interest, 164
  covenants not-to-compete, 165
  employment agreement, 165
  indemnification and resolution of disputes, 164

obligations of buyer and
seller, 164
termination and
abandonment, 165
trades act secrets, 165
undisclosed liabilities, 164
Pygmalion (Shaw), 134

Rate of capitalization: *see* Cap
rates
Real estate, 92–94
leasing from seller, 93–94
Rent, 62
Repairs, 62
Replacement cost, 71
Richard Kittson & Company,
124–25
Rockne, Knute, 172
Rogers, Will (quoted), 125, 169
Royalties, 99

Salaries, 59
Sales:
factors affecting, 178
forecast, 178
questions in due diligence,
195
trends, 177
Sales and marketing, 173–74
Sales value, comparable, 71–72
Scientific and photographic
equipment businesses, 36
Section 369 "tax-loss
carry-forward," 155
Sellers:
dealing with after you own,
170–71
elicit key concerns, 143
establish positive relationship
with, 138–39
obligations in purchase and
sale agreement, 164

putting at ease, 143
qualify, how to, 141–43
Sellers remorse, 140–41
Semiconductor and related
devices industry, 36
Service station businesses, 36
Seymour Pollock & Associates,
124
Shareholders, 179
Shaw, George Bernard:
Pygmalion by, 134
Standard & Poor, 28
Standard Rate & Data Service,
21
address, 37
Strategy statement:
in financial package, 124,
125
operating tactics in, 125
Suppliers:
dealing with in liquidation,
13
key or dominant, 52–53
source of leads, 31–32
Supplies, 62

Talcott Associates, 114
Tax Reform Act of 1986, 155
Taxes, 62
Telephone, 62
Telephone calls, 30–31
sample script, 31
Termination and abandonment,
165
Thomas Publishing Company,
28
address, 38
*Thomas Register of American
Manufacturers,* 38
Times Mirror Press (address),
38
tobacco wholesaler businesses,
35

Trade associations, 23, 37
Trade journals, 21–23
   questions to ask, 22–23
   run classified ads in, 26–27
Trades act secrets, 165
Transportation equipment
   manufacturing businesses,
   36
Travel and entertainment, 62–63
Triple net, CPI lease, 93
Trust security account, 104–105
Trust security agreement, 160
Turner, Ted, 3, 104, 105

Uniform Commercial Code, 64
   Bulk Sales Act, 160, 162
Unions, 180
United States Department of
   Commerce, 23
   address, 37

United States Treasury bonds,
   110
U.S. Industrial Outlook, 23
Utilities, 62

Venture, 23

Wall Street Journal, 23, 26, 27,
   114
Westinghouse Credit, 114
Wood products manufacturing
   businesses, 36

X-ray apparatus and tubes
   industry, 36

Zero coupon bonds, 98–99, 110